Mock Applique'

By Sara Nephew

Dedication

To Derek and Tracy, and to Taylor, our pretty flower.

Acknowledgments

Quilters are generous. Sincere thanks to those who were willing to test the patterns for this book: Annette Austin, Diane Coombs, Joan Dawson, Rose Herrera, Mary Pierce, Terri Shinn, Kathleen Springer, and Lynn Williams.

Thanks also to the skilled quilters who came to my help against the pressure of deadlines: Annette Austin, Lynne Baxter, Connie Buss, Nadine Darby, Joan Dawson, Rose Herrera, Lynn Williams, and Penny Wolf.

Credits

Photography by Carl Murray
Graphics and cover by Elizabeth Nephew
All quilts in this book have been designed and pieced by Sara Nephew unless otherwise noted.

Mock Applique' ©

Clearview Triangle

8311 180th St. S.E.
Snohomish, WA 98290-4802 USA

Library of Congress Catalog Card Number 95-67105
ISBN 0-9621172-4-2

Contents

Preface

In a previous book ("Stars and Flowers: Three-Sided Patchwork") I played with designs with the idea of making a feathered star quilt from 60° triangles. Surprisingly some of the resulting quilts looked more like floral applique' than stars. This is a pleasant effect of equilateral designs--they often remind us of botanical forms, since flowers and leaves often grow in groups of three, six, nine, etc. These are the inevitable groupings of equilateral shapes. Also nature uses some of these shapes, like 60° triangles and hexagons to add strength to living structures. They are found all around us, if we look.

Even after the book was finished, designs with a Floral Applique' look kept showing up on the equilateral graph paper. These are my favorite of all the quilt designs I've done. Perhaps they are loved because of the connection to traditional designs. Yet wrapping up in beautiful flowers says something about the value of a person. The image is rich in poetic meaning. The quilt means warmth and caring, and flowers add beauty and elegance. A powerful addition to daily life!

Use your Sewing Machine

For quilters who admire floral applique', but have no desire to do so much hand stitching, these rotary cut and machine pieced quilts quickly gratify the desire to wrap up in flower and fruit designs. Some may prefer this kind of design (a combination of floral theme and geometric precision) to freewheeling applique'.

Or those who love to hand stitch may wish to **add** applique' to these quilt designs. There is enough space left in many of the quilts to accommodate the addition, and it seems the resulting patterns would be very rich in design and extremely floral looking.

Whether you love applique' or prefer the geometry of piecing I hope you enjoy quickly making these quilts for your beds or your walls.

Fabric Choices

To increase the floral illusion of these designs, it is often best to use strong light and dark contrasts between the background fabric and the floral shapes. This is the same technique used in traditional applique, where red, green, and even black fabrics were often used against a muslin or white background.

Use of these traditional color schemes increases the floral applique' look. Use of a light background with any strong colors is generally successful. Or a very dark background with lighter colored fabrics for the design is also pleasing. (Example: CHERRIES, pg.38)

Small prints and solids help hold the shapes together, while large prints and less contrast will tend to break up the pattern of a flower or a leaf. The adventurous quilter may wish to experiment with large prints and ambiguous value choices to achieve a more painterly effect. (Example: PINEAPPLE QUILT, pg.33)

Quilting Makes it Beautiful

For those who love to quilt, large areas of light plain background fabric look gorgeous covered with fancy hand quilting. Some of the quilts in this book were finished this way, and they deserved every stitch.

A good choice for a quilting pattern for Mock Applique' would be a design with curves, since the piecing is geometric. You may wish to quilt a curved leaf over a green diamond, to soften the shape and add to the illusion. A traditional applique' pattern that's well-rounded would be a great choice to adapt for quilting. For example, a rose applique' pattern was used for quilting ENGLISH ROSE. Of course, feathers are always beautifully rounded and can be made to fit in any space.

Something Different

For those in a hurry, I was thrilled to discover another approach to quilting. A number of the pattern testers for this book chose a busy printed background fabric that was still light enough to contrast well with the block design. The background was then machine quilted (a big commercial machine) in an all over meander design. This leaves some hand quilting on the blocks and borders, but the amount of work is minimal, compared to the traditional approach. Costs are usually quite reasonable. Plan the scale of the quilted meander to match the scale of the pattern pieces, so the quilting texture is consistent over all.

Contrast Increases Floral Illusion

Quilting Pattern for English Rose

Towards a More Perfect Quilt

The Mock Applique' quilt is worthy of your best efforts. Careful piecing will result in an heirloom quilt that can be treasured for generations. Accurate rotary cutting and some concentration on a ¼" seam will help assure beautifully shaped leaves and flowers.

Please be careful to trim the seam edges of dark fabrics that may show through light backgrounds at crucial spots. Also do follow the piecing tips for trimming half-diamonds and half-triangles as shown in the diagrams on pg.10 and pg.13. You'll be glad you did!

New Rules

The rules and tables of measurement given in each book have occasionally changed slightly here or there. Perhaps a new shape was given to cut, or a better method has been discovered to cut an old shape. Rarely a correction to a measurement makes it easier to piece units. So my cutting method has evolved slightly.

Always the newest book has the most up-to-date version of the cutting directions. It may be to the quilter's advantage to always use the newest directions and methods, even when working on a pattern from an older book.

Introduction

This book is designed as a workbook with complete piecing directions given for 16 quilts. In the beginning all the directions are given for Clearview Triangle cutting methods, with information about changing the sizes of the patterns, trimming tips, how to cut extra-large pieces, etc. You may wish to read through this section to become familiar with the cutting, or as a review.

Or you may wish to go directly to the patterns, especially if you have pieced Clearview Triangle quilts before. If don't remember how to cut a particular shape, the index on pg. 71 will quickly direct you to the page that has the help you need.

The author has made an effort in this book to include even more specific cutting directions within individual patterns. So you should need to turn less often to the front pages for help, making it easier and more fun to piece these quilts.

Tools

Two key tools go a long way in saving time when making these quilts. The Clearview Triangle makes rotary cutting and accurate piecing of 60° triangles, 60° diamonds, hexagons, etc., fast and easy. The triangle comes in three sizes. The Half-Diamond is designed especially for rotary cutting speed-pieced 60° diamonds divided lengthwise into two different fabrics. It also speeds the cutting of some other shapes. These tools are made from ⅛" acrylic, for use with a rotary cutter. (See pg. 72 for ordering information.)

Besides Clearview Triangles, required tools are: rotary cutter, mat, and a straight ruler like Omnigrid for cutting strips. A large rotary cutter is preferred, since it saves muscle strain, cuts faster, and tends to stay on a straight line. A 6" x 12" ruler moves less while cutting.

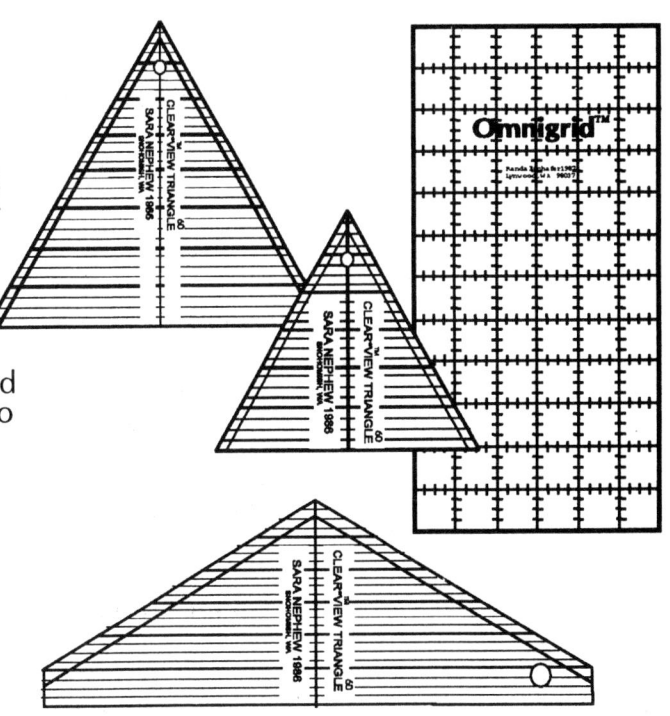

Rotary Cutting and Speed Piecing

These cutting methods are based on:
1. a strip of fabric;
2. a plastic triangle with a ruled line on the perpendicular.

The triangle is laid on the strip in various ways, and a rotary cutter is used to cut off portions of the fabric strip.

Nothing in this book is difficult to do as long as the triangle and the strip are kept in mind. The strip may be changed by making it wider or narrower, or by sewing it to another strip before doing any cutting. The triangle may be changed by making it larger or smaller, or by changing it from a 60° (equilateral) triangle to a 120° half-diamond.

By working just with these elements, many shapes can be cut in whatever size desired. These shapes will all fit together to form a design, a quilt top.

After piecing a large number of these quilts, I have found that it is not necessary to calculate all measurements each time a new design is cut and pieced. Instead, knowledge of a few basic rules often makes the next step automatic.

The following section lists the rules and the methods for cutting various shapes. You may wish to read through the whole section before beginning to piece any of the patterns in this book. The index at the back of the book makes it easy to find a shape so you can review cutting methods while piecing a particular pattern.

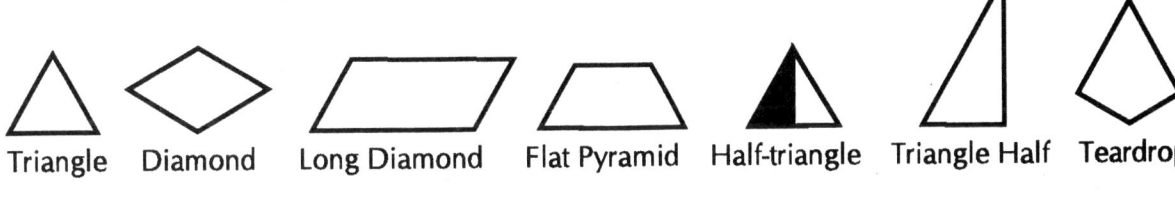

Triangle   Diamond   Long Diamond   Flat Pyramid   Half-triangle   Triangle Half   Teardrop

 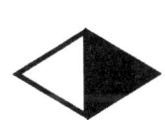    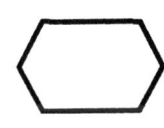

Quarter Hex   Matching Triangle   Half-diamond   Diamond Half   Hexagon   Gem   Long Hex

Cutting Strips

The first step in cutting any shape is cutting strips. All fabric should be prewashed. 100% cotton is preferred.

1. Fold fabric selvage to selvage and press. If pressing from the selvage to the fold produces wrinkles, move the top layer of fabric left or right keeping selvages parallel, until wrinkles disappear.
2. Bring fold to selvage (folding again) and press.
3. Use the wide ruler as a right angle guide, or line up the selvages with the edge of the mat, and the ruler with the mat edge perpendicular to the selvage. Cut off the ragged or irregular edges of the fabric.
4. Cut the strip width required, using the newly trimmed fabric edge as a guide.
5. Open the strip. It should be straight, not zig zag. Adjust the ruler if necessary and trim fabric edges slightly before cutting the next strip.

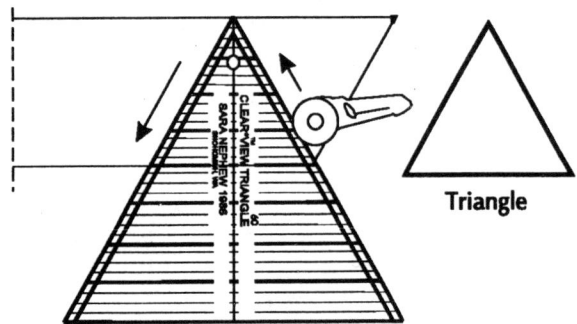

Triangle

Rules

1. Before beginning to cut and piece any design, a **triangle size** is chosen to determine the scale of the design. (A **triangle size** is given for each pattern.)

2. A triangle is cut from a strip whose width is the same as the triangle's height.

3. Diamonds, long diamonds, quarter hexes, and flat pyramids are cut from a strip ¼" narrower than the strip a triangle is cut from.

4. Half-triangles and triangle halves are cut from a strip ½" wider than the strip a triangle is cut from.

All of the rules and measurements in this book apply if a ¼" seam is taken.

Cutting Directions

The cutting directions in this book are essentially the same as those in my previous books. A few changes and improvements have been made. Some of the shapes that can be cut are not needed in these patterns; but the directions remain for those who may devise a design requiring these shapes.

To cut triangles:
Rule: a triangle is cut from a strip whose width is the same as the triangle's height. (A 3" triangle is cut from a 3" strip.)
1. Position the tip of the Clearview Triangle at one edge of the strip and the proper ruled line at the other edge of the strip.
2. Rotary cut along the 2 sides of the triangle. Move the tool along the same edge (do not flip it to the other side of the fabric strip) for the next cut. Line up the tool again as shown.
3. Cut along both sides of the triangle. Strips may be stacked up to 8 thicknesses and all cut at once.

To cut diamonds:

Rule: Diamonds, long diamonds, flat pyramids, and quarter hexes are cut from a strip ¼" narrower than the strip a triangle is cut from.

1. Position the Clearview Triangle with one side along one edge of the strip. Cut the end of the strip to a 60° angle.
2. Reposition the Clearview Triangle so the tip is at one edge of the strip and a ruled line is along the other edge. (The same position as is used to cut triangles, except the strip is ¼" narrower.) Rotary cut **only** along the side away from the first cut.
3. Keep moving the tool along the same side of the strip, lining up the cut edge and the side of the tool as shown. Always cut the side away from the first cut. (Strips may be stacked up to eight thickness' and all cut at once.)

To cut long diamonds and flat pyramids:

Rule: Diamonds, long diamonds, flat pyramids, and quarter hexes are cut from a strip ¼" narrower than the strip a triangle is cut from.

Method #1

Trim one end of the strip to a 60° angle. Sew long side of the strip to the piece desired. Trim other end to correct angle.

Method #2 (Long Diamond)

1. Trim one end of the strip to 60° angle.
2. Place the Clearview Triangle over the fabric strip, with a 60° fabric triangle extending from under the tool, as shown at right. Set the bottom edge of the strip at the measurement given in the pattern, or according to the TABLE OF COMMON SHAPES (pg. 18). Cut the side away from the first cut.

Method #3 (Flat Pyramid)

Place the Clearview Triangle over the fabric strip, lining up one edge of the strip at the measurement given in the pattern, or according to the TABLE OF COMMON SHAPES. Cut each side of the strip.

Note: care must be taken when cutting long diamonds, as they do have a reverse of their shape, Check carefully to be sure you are cutting them in the direction required by the pattern. If you don't need both the long diamond and its reverse, keep fabric right sides up. Try cutting just one first, to be sure it's right.

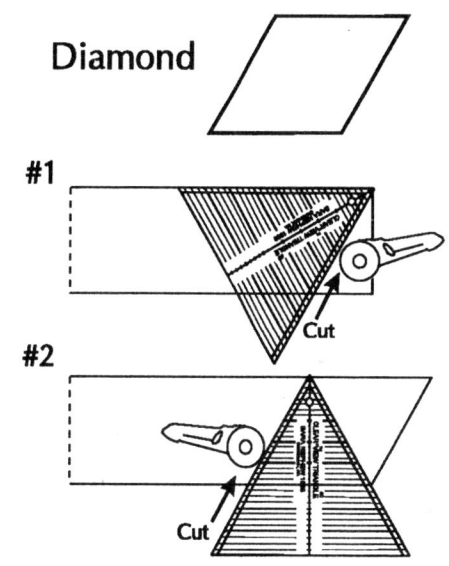

Diamond

#1
#2

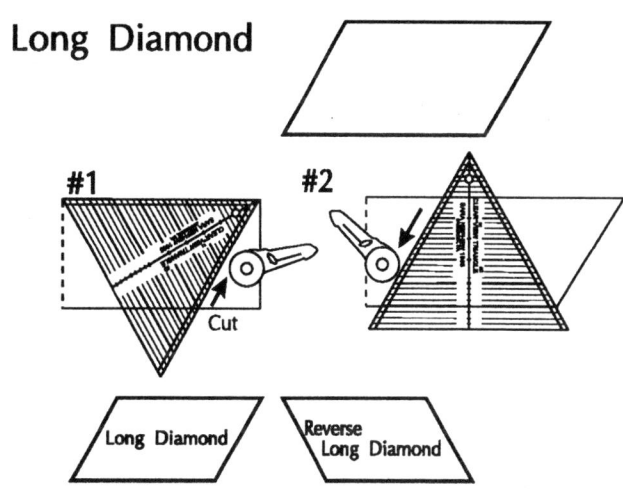

Long Diamond

#1 #2

Long Diamond   Reverse Long Diamond

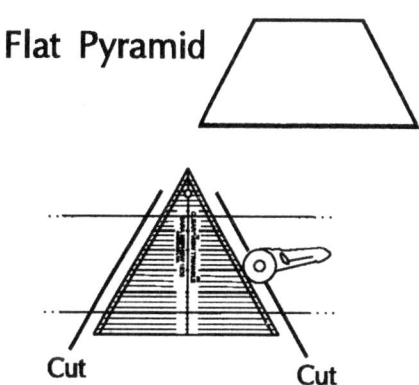

Flat Pyramid

Cut   Cut

Quarter Hexagon

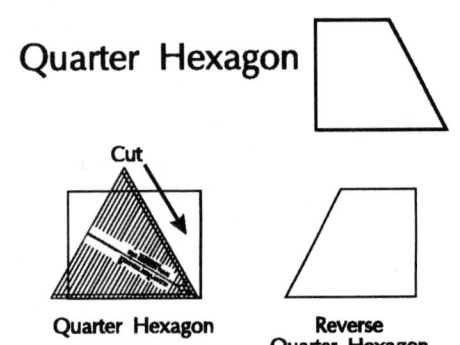

Quarter Hexagon

Reverse Quarter Hexagon

To cut a quarter hex:
Rule: Diamonds, long diamonds, flat pyramids, and quarter hexes are cut from a strip ¼" narrower than the strip a triangle is cut from.
1. Cut the strip into rectangles according to the table below.
2. Position the Clearview Triangle with one side along one edge of the strip. Cut the end of the strip to a 60° angle.

Triangle Size	Strip Width	Rectangle
2"	1¾"	2⅛"
3"	2¾"	3⅜"
4"	3¾"	4½"
5"	4¾"	5⅝"
6"	5¾"	6⅞"

Triangle Half

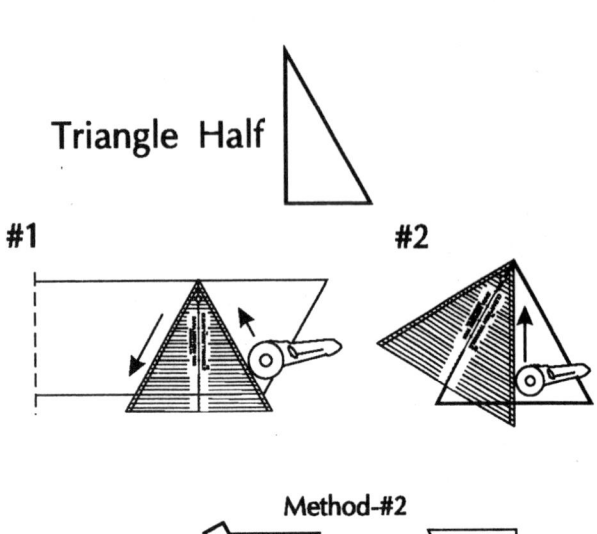

#1

#2

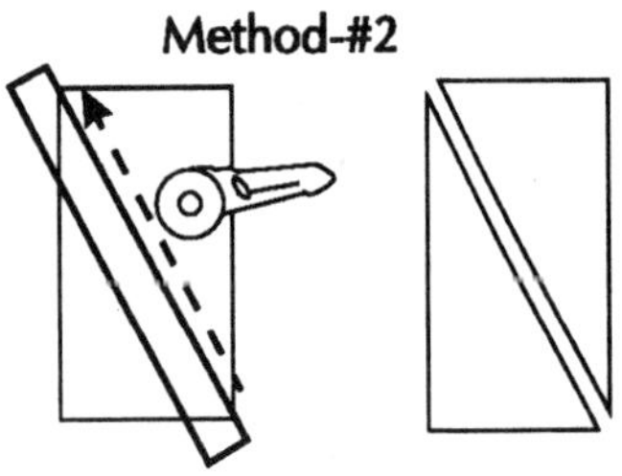

Method-#2

To cut a triangle half:
Rule: Half-triangles and triangle halves are cut from a strip ½" wider than the strip a triangle is cut from.

Method #1
1. Cut triangles from a strip ½" wider than the basic triangle size.
2. Line up the side of the fabric triangle with the center line of the Clearview Triangle, then cut the fabric triangle in half along the ruler edge.

Method #2
Cut a rectangle the height needed for the triangle half and half the width of that triangle's base (measure with a ruler). Then bisect this rectangle from corner to corner diagonally. This will produce two halves the same, rather than left and right.

To cut a diamond half:

Method #1
Use the Clearview Half-Diamond to rotary cut 120° triangles from the proper width strip. (See the table of measurements for half-diamonds on page 16.)

Method #2
1. Line up the center line of the Clearview Triangle with edge of fabric strip. Cut along edge of tool.
2. Flip tool, line up the center line with strip edge and line up previous cut at edge of tool. Cut other 30° angle.

Diamond Half

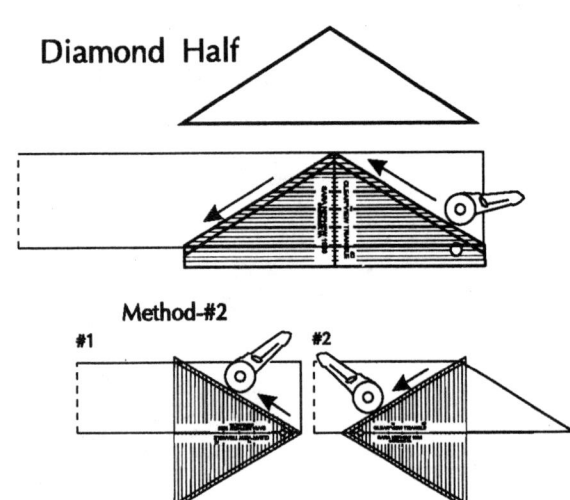

Method-#2

#1

#2

Teardrop Unit

A teardrop unit, made from one teardrop shape and two triangle halves, is very useful. Triangle halves are cut from a strip ½" bigger than the strip a triangle is cut from. Teardrops are cut from strip widths according to the table below. Seam one triangle half on each side of the teardrop to make a diamond-shaped unit. Line these pieces up for seaming at the bottom, not the top. Press each seam to the triangle half. Trim off the little seam ears to finish.

To cut a teardrop:

1. Cut a fabric strip according to the pattern directions, or according to the teardrop table below.

Triangle size	Strip to cut
2"	2¼"
3"	3⅜"
4"	4½"
5"	5⅝"
6"	6¾"

2. Cut triangles from the strip.

Method #1

1. Position Clearview Half-Diamond on triangle so its tip is opposite triangle tip. Line up the fabric triangle point with the perpendicular line of the tool and line the fabric triangle sides up evenly with one of the rulings, as shown. Make sure the tip of the tool is inside the base of the fabric triangle. Then use rotary cutter to trim off the extra fabric and make a teardrop.

Method #2

1. Cut fabric triangles as #1 above.

2. Measure the base of these triangles and find the center point.

3. Lay the center line of a 60° Clearview Triangle along the base of the fabric triangle, with the point at center. Rotary cut this wedge off. Reverse the tool and cut off the other wedge.

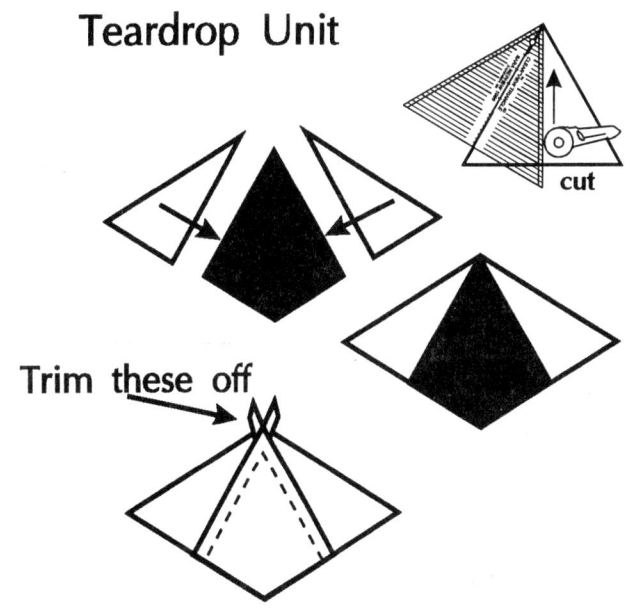

Teardrop Unit

Trim these off

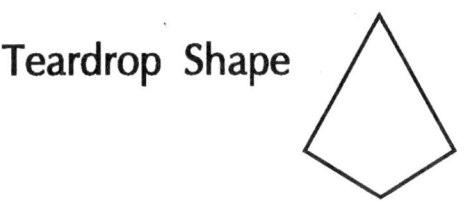

Teardrop Shape

Cut Teardrop Method-#1

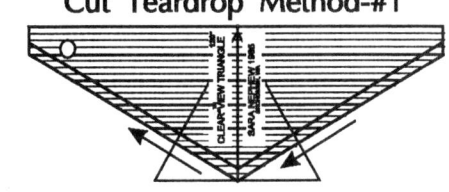

Method-#2

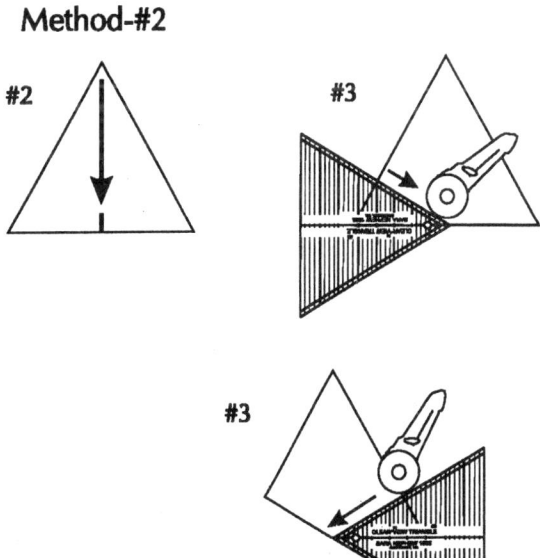

Hexagon

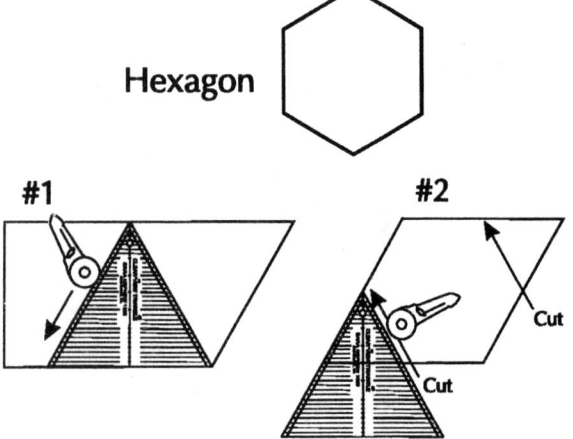

#1   #2

Cut

Cut

To cut a hexagon:
1. Cut a fabric strip according to pattern, or according to hexagon table below.
2. Cut 60° diamonds from the strip. (See "to cut diamonds," pg. 9).
3. From each end of the diamonds, cut a triangle whose size is half of the strip width.

To cut a gem shape:
Instead of cutting a hexagon from the diamond, cut only one point off, leaving this shape.

HEXAGON TABLE

Triangle size	Strip to cut	Cut off triangle
2"	3"	1½"
3"	5"	2½"
4"	7"	3½"
5"	9"	4½"
6"	11"	5½"

Gem Shape

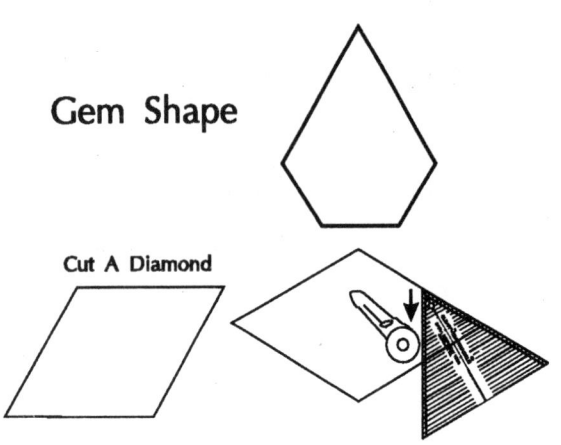

Cut A Diamond

To cut a long hex:
1. Cut a strip width according to the HEXAGON TABLE.
2. Cut a long diamond (see pg. 9). Push the ruler up to the correct measurement below.
3. From each end of the long diamond, cut a triangle whose size is ½ of the strip width.

Triangle Size	Side Length
2"	4¼"
3"	7¼"
4"	9¾"

Long Hexagon

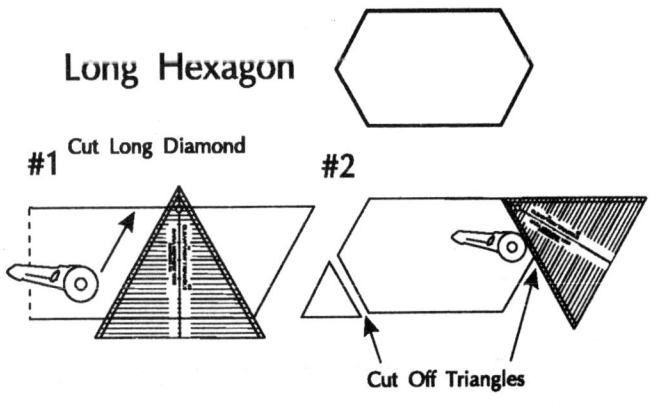

#1   Cut Long Diamond   #2

Cut Off Triangles

Sandwich Piecing

Sandwich piecing is a speed technique which uses two presewn strips of fabric.

To sandwich piece matching triangle units:
1. Cut strips of fabric the width of the triangle size. Two different fabrics are used, usually one light and one dark. Seam these strips right sides together with a ¼" seam down both the right and the left side of the pair of strips.
2. Position the Clearview Triangle so the tip is at one edge of the strips, and the ruled line for the correct size triangle at the other edge. Rotary cut on both sides of the tool. (Same as cutting triangles.) Pull the tips of the seamed triangles apart and press open.

Matching Triangle

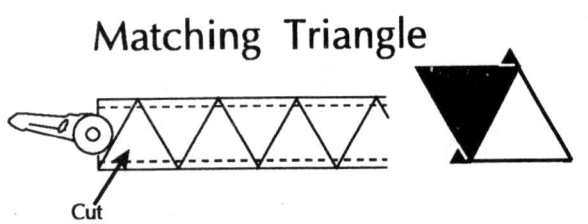

Cut

To sandwich piece half-diamond units:

1. Cut strips of fabric according to the pattern, or according to the half-diamond table. Two fabrics are used, usually one light and one dark.
2. Sew strips right sides together with a ¼" seam allowance down each side.
3. **Method #1**
   Using a Clearview Half-Diamond and a rotary cutter, cut triangles from the seamed strips. Line up ruler tip at one edge, and the desired line on the ruler at the other edge, and cut both sides.
   Method #2
   Line up the center line of the Clearview Triangle with edge of fabric strip. Cut along edge of tool. Flip tool, line up the center line with strip edge and line up previous cut at edge of tool. Cut other 30° angle.
4. Use a seam ripper to cut one stitch at the seamed tip of the fabric 120° triangles. Pull the tips of the seamed triangles apart and press open, pressing to the dark across the width of the diamond and pulling the top and bottom out straight while pressing. Trim off little seam ears as shown.

HALF-DIAMOND TABLE

Triangle Size	Strip Width
2"	1¼"
3"	1⅞"
4"	2⅜"
5"	3"
6"	3½"

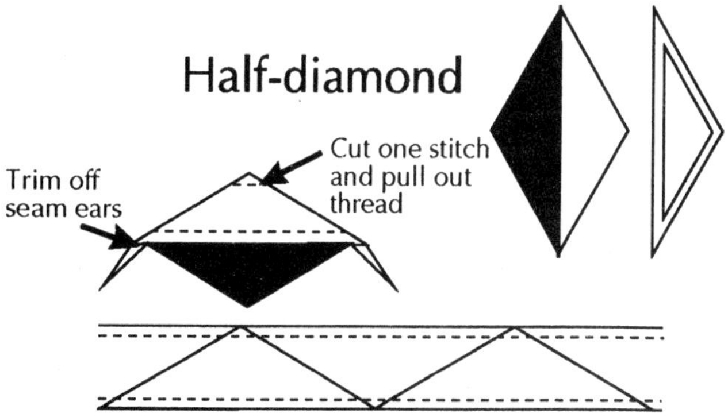

Half-diamond

Trim off seam ears

Cut one stitch and pull out thread

To sandwich piece half-triangle units:

Rule: Half-triangles and triangle halves are cut from a strip ½" wider than the strip a triangle is cut from. *Note: this rule is being applied in a different way in these new improved directions.*

1. Cut two fabric strips according to the pattern, or according to the HALF-TRIANGLE TABLE. Usually a dark and a light are used. Sew these right sides together, with a ¼" seam down both sides.
2. Cut seamed strips into sections according to the table or ½" bigger than the triangle size.
3. Bisect sections diagonally by lining up the center line of the Clearview Triangle along one long edge at the correct measurement, and cutting. Turn the remaining half and line up the triangle again to check accuracy, trimming as necessary. This produces two left or two right half-triangles. To obtain the reverse, flip section over so other fabric is up.

HALF-TRIANGLE TABLE

Triangle Size	Strip Width	Cut into sections
2"	1½"	2½"
3"	2"	3½"
4"	2⅝"	4½"
5"	3⅜"	5½"
6"	3¾"	6½"

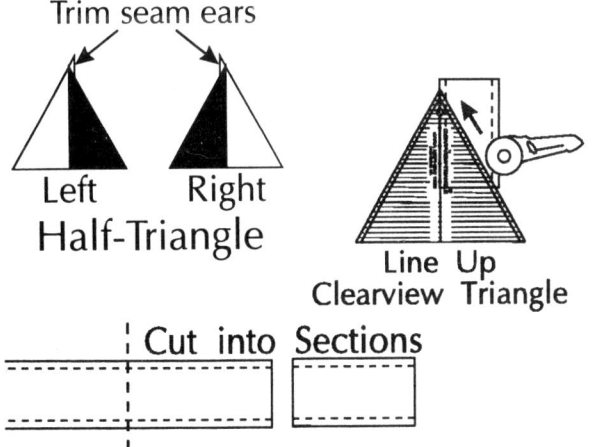

Trim seam ears

Left   Right
Half-Triangle

Line Up Clearview Triangle

Cut into Sections

Cutting a Large Triangle
Method #1

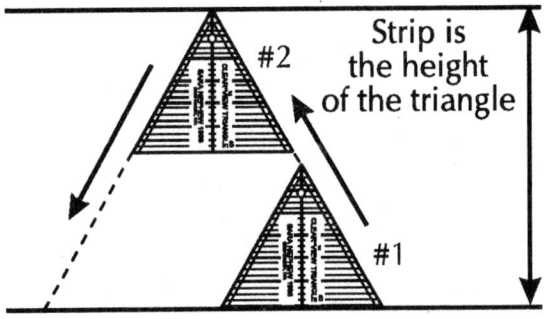

Strip is the height of the triangle

Method #2

cut

cut

Extend the edge with a long ruler

Fabric Edge

Cutting a Large Diamond Half
Method #1

#3

#2

#1

Put triangle on pencil line

Mark with a pencil line

Cutting a Large Flat Pyramid
Method #1

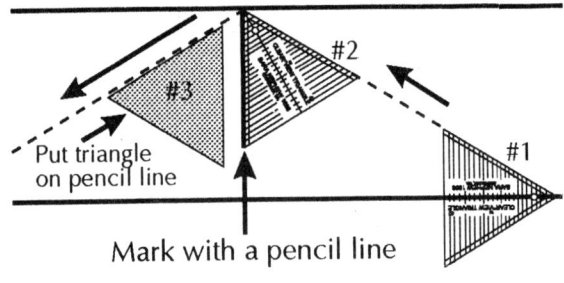

cut

Cutting Large Shapes

No matter how large a Clearview Triangle you are using, sooner or later you will find yourself faced with the task of cutting a shape even larger. Don't be intimidated by the idea. Remember, you are dealing with only a small number of possible angles in 60° quilts (30°, 60°, or 120°), and they are easy to recognize. There are two relatively simple ways to approach this cutting challenge.

First Method

If a triangle is needed, the first solution is to cut a strip the height of the triangle. Then cut the angles needed. If you are cutting a large equilateral triangle (60° at all three corners) use the Clearview Triangle to get an accurate angle at the first corner. Then either extend the side line with a long straight ruler or move the Clearview Triangle along the cut edge to continue. Cut the next corner accurately and continue until the shape is finished.

For a large diamond half (30° at left and right and 120° at the top) use the center line of the Clearview Triangle to get the 30° angle needed at the first corner. After cutting to the top, mark a line on the fabric lightly with chalk or washout marker along the inner edge of the tool. Move the Clearview Triangle to the other side of this line (two 60's make 120°) and begin to cut the last side of the half-diamond. Use the center line on the last corner again to assure accuracy.

Remember, the larger the piece you are cutting, the less difference *small* variations will make to the units' comfortable fit in the quilt top.

Second Method

The second approach is to add ruler height to the Clearview Triangle that you have in order to make it a larger triangle (sort of). To cut a large triangle out of any piece of fabric, first make a straight cut along one edge of the fabric. Put the base of the Clearview Triangle on this straight fabric edge. Then use a ruler to add the necessary inches, pushing the triangle tool up. Cut the left and right sides by either laying a straightedge down or by moving the Clear-view Triangle and continuing the cut as above.

Adding inches with a ruler is how to cut an extra-large flat pyramid. Strip width is given in the pattern. The Clearview Triangle is placed over the strip, with the base at the bottom edge of the strip. Again use a ruler to add the necessary inches, pushing the triangle tool up. Cut left and right sides as above.

Enlarging or Shrinking a Pattern

It's fun to try substituting a different triangle size when piecing a particular quilt design. Following are instructions on how to do a rough estimate of how altering triangle size will change the size of the quilt. (To calculate new dimensions exactly, see pg. 17.)

The perpendicular triangle measurement is easy to figure. Just subtract ¾" from the triangle size chosen to obtain "finished" height and multiply by the number of triangles perpendicular across the grid of the quilt design. (If this is not easily seen, sketch the design on graph paper.)

By comparing the new measure-measurement with the original, you can then estimate the other dimension of the quilt. Changing to a 2" triangle size from a 3" triangle size results in a quilt about ¼ the size. Changing to a 4" triangle size from a 3" triangle size results in a quilt about ⅓ larger.

To substitute a new triangle size follow the RULES and CUTTING DIRECTIONS for all the standard pieces. For larger pieces, or for flat pyramids, etc. the following information and table will be helpful. Use this information to change the size of shapes or to find the size of a shape in an original design.

When a shape is on graph paper, it can be analyzed and its size determined using simple math. Count the rows in the shape.

Example: (All the math in this example is based on a 3" triangle size.) The gridded triangle at the right is composed of a triangle and a flat pyramid. The triangle is cut from a 3" strip, loses ¼" seam when sewn to the flat pyramid. the flat pyramid is cut from a 2¾" strip, and loses ¼" seam when sewn to the triangle.

Result: 2¾" triangle height plus 2½" flat pyramid height equals 5¼", so this shape is cut at 5¼" line on Clearview Triangle.

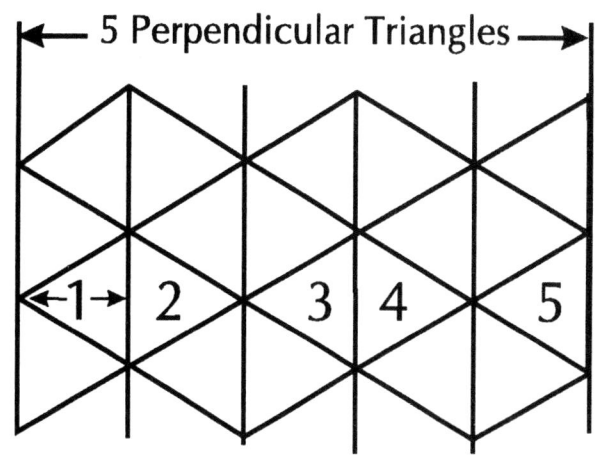

← 5 Perpendicular Triangles →

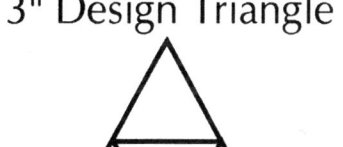

3" Design Triangle

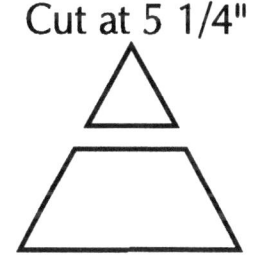

Cut at 5 1/4"

COMMON SHAPES

Design Triangle size | Use this base line on the Clearview Triangle
2" | 3¼"
3" | 5¼"
4" | 7¼"
5" | 9¼"
6" | 11¼"

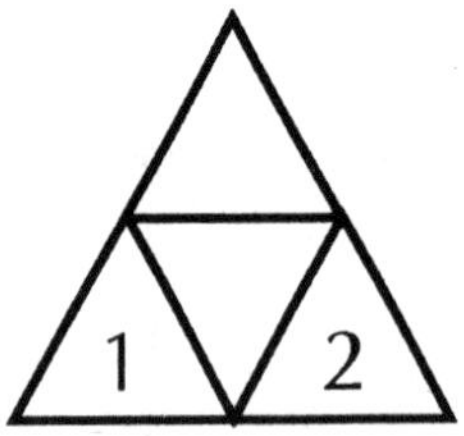

Design Triangle size | Use this base line on the Clearview Triangle
2" | 4½"
3" | 7½"
4" | 10½"
5" | 13½"
6" | 16½"

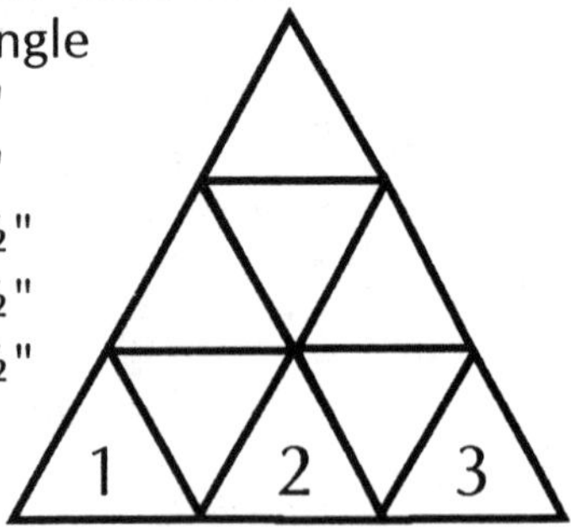

Base

Design Triangle size | Use this base line on the Clearview Triangle
2" | 5¾"
3" | 9¾"
4" | 13¾"
5" | 17¾"
6" | 21¾"

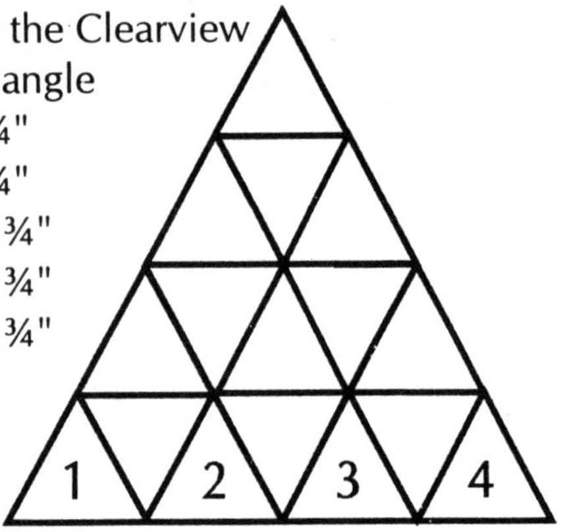

Base

Design Triangle size | Use this base line on the Clearview Triangle
2" | 3¼"
3" | 5¼"
4" | 7¼"
5" | 9¼"
6" | 11¼"

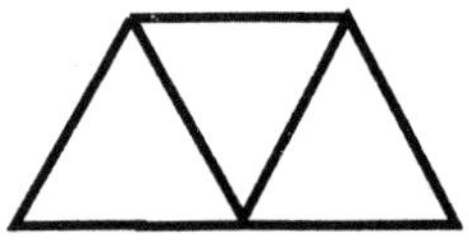

Base

Design Triangle size | Use this base line on the Clearview Triangle
2" | 4½"
3" | 7½"
4" | 10½"
5" | 13½"
6" | 16½"

Base

Design Triangle size | Use this base line on the Clearview Triangle
2" | 3"
3" | 5"
4" | 7"
5" | 9"
6" | 11"

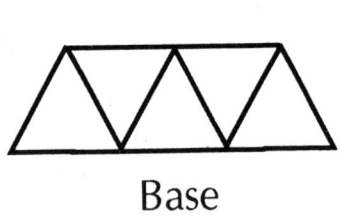

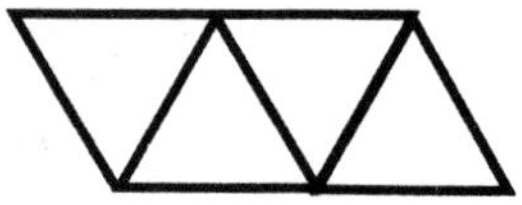

or

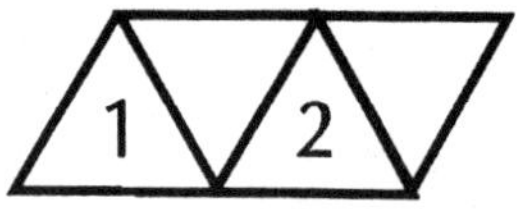

PIECES PER STRIP TABLE

Approximate yield per 42" pre-shrunk strip of fabric for the most popular pattern sizes.

SHAPE	triangle size 2"	3"	4"
triangle, matching triangle	31	19	16
diamond	19	12	8-9
triangle halves, half-triangles	16	11	9
half-diamond, diamond half	17	11	9
standard long diamond	11	6	4
standard flat pyramid	14	8	5
hexagon, gem	11	6	4
teardrop	27	19	10
long hex	7	4	2
quarter hex	19	12	9

ABOUT THESE QUILTS

As in all my books, these patterns are arranged somewhat in order of difficulty, with the easy quilts at the front of the book and the more challenging designs at the back. If you've never used these cutting methods or the tools before, you may wish to first try one of the patterns near the front.

The author has tried to give more complete cutting directions with each pattern than ever before, but if the piece requires a more complex explanation, or if the quilter is unfamiliar with the cutting methods, you will need to turn to the cutting directions at the front of the book. See the index on pg. 71 for the needed page numbers.

Changing the Size of a Quilt

Each pattern begins with the triangle size that determines the scale of the whole design. Advanced piecers can change this triangle size and then apply the tables and rules in the pages of cutting directions to cut the whole quilt design to a different size.

When changing the size/scale of a quilt, you can determine the finished dimensions of the pattern portion of the quilt by counting the number of triangles in one perpendicular line across the pattern and multiplying times the correct perpendicular measurement below. Then count the number of triangle sides across the other direction of the pattern, times the correct side length below. This will give you the new length and width.

TABLE OF FINISHED TRIANGLES

(when using ¼' seams)

Triangle Size	Finished Perpendicular	Finished Side Length
2"	1¼"	1$^7/_{16}$"
3"	2¼"	2$^5/_8$"
4"	3¼"	3$^{13}/_{16}$"
5"	4¼"	4$^{15}/_{16}$"
6"	5¼"	6$^1/_8$"

SHAMROCK
4½" triangle size
Quilt with borders: 61" x 75"

All fabric prewashed 42" wide.
Fabric requirements:
4 yds. muslin
1¾ yds. assorted thirties prints

Directions:
1. Cut for one block (36 blocks altogether):
* 3 muslin teardrops from a 5¼" strip (108 altogether)
* 1 muslin 4½" triangle (33 altogether)
* 3 print or color teardrops from a 5¼" strip (108 altogether)

(You may wish to substitute colored teardrops for muslin teardrops in some blocks, so these numbers may vary.)

2. Sew the teardrops three and three as shown, pressing seams as indicated. Then sew across the middle to make the Shamrock leaves. Add a 4½" muslin triangle at the top right as shown. Make three blocks substituting 5" muslin triangle halves cut from a 5" muslin triangle for the 4½" muslin triangle (A).

3. To make the stem triangle: (36 will be needed) Cut muslin rectangles 2⅞" x 5". Use the Clearview Triangle to make an accurate diagonal cut as shown, trimming as necessary. Cut two green strips 1" wide and one muslin strip 2⅜" wide. Sew into a set of strips as shown. Cut into rectangles 5" high. Place the Clearview Triangle along one long edge and cut the triangle half as shown. Turn and trim the waste from the other triangle half. Pull off the little green tip. Sew this stem triangle half to the muslin triangle half to make the stem triangle. Sew onto the bottom left of the leaves. This completes the shamrock block.

4. To assemble the quilt top: Make six rows of six blocks each. Finish three rows at the top with the three (A) blocks above, and at the bottom with 8½" x 11" muslin rectangles trimmed to a 60° angle as shown. Finish the other three rows at the top with 8½" x 8" muslin rectangles trimmed to a 60° angle as shown, and at the bottom with muslin triangle halves cut from 9" triangles. Line up the diagonal seams when the vertical rows are sewn together, and then trim the fill-in pieces at the top and bottom edges as necessary. Terry added a 2½" inner muslin border, a 2" scrappy 30's print border, and a 4¾" final muslin border.

2.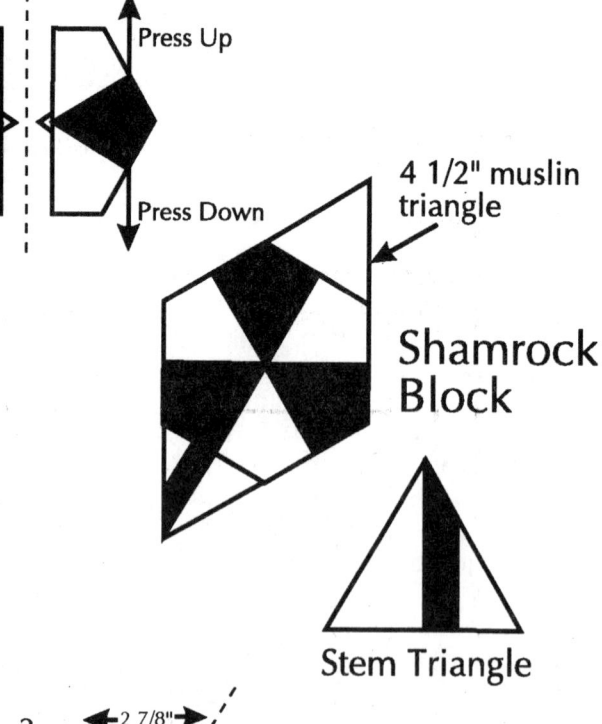

Press Up

Press Down

4 1/2" muslin triangle

Shamrock Block

Stem Triangle

3.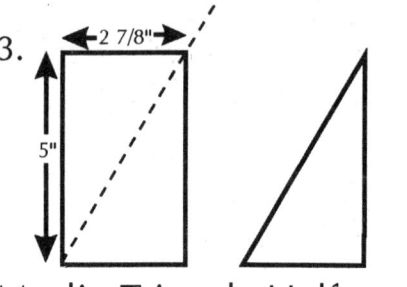

Muslin Triangle Half

3. Set of Strips Cut into Sections

3. Waste

Center line of Clearview Triangle

Stem Triangle Half

4.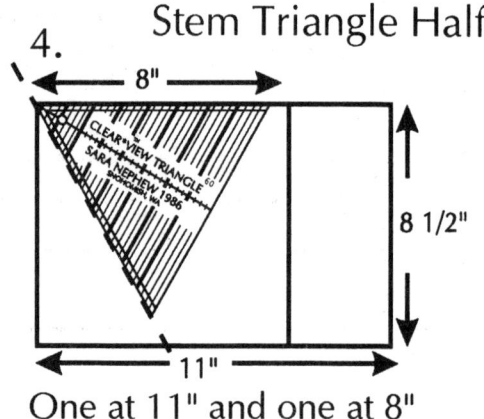

One at 11" and one at 8"

Shamrock

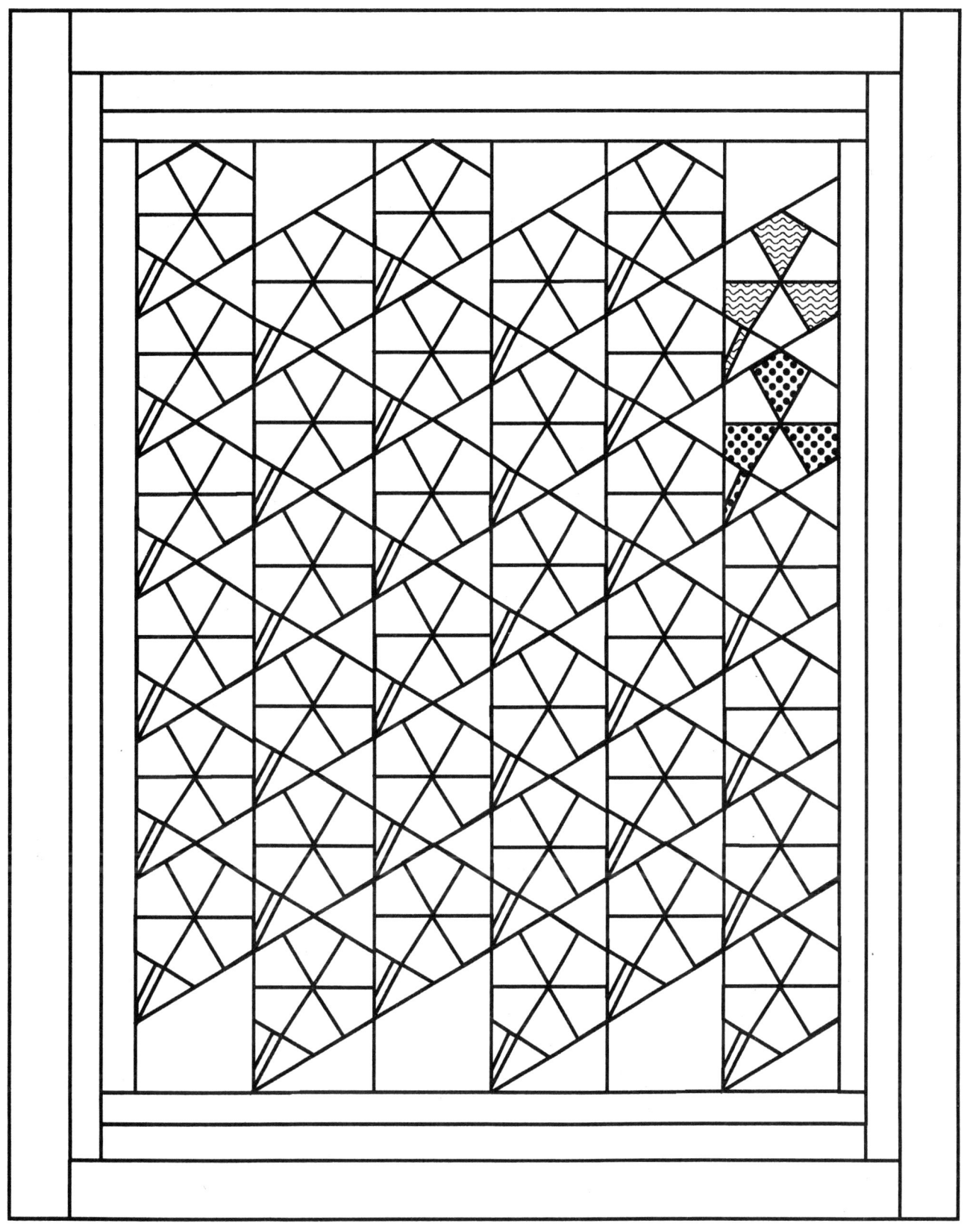

PINEAPPLE QUILT

4" triangle size
Quilt with borders: 60½" x 67½"
All fabric prewashed 42" wide.
Fabric requirements:
¼ yd. dark green
1¾ yd. background fabric
1½ yd. total mixed pineapple colors (strips or scraps)
¾ yd. large print for final left and right borders

Directions:

1. Sandwich piece 24 half-diamonds from 2⅜" dark green and background fabric set(s) of strips. Sandwich piece six left and six right half-triangles from a 2⅜" dark green and background fabric set of strips.

2. In addition, cut for each block:
- 2 background 4" triangles
- 1 background diamond from a 3¾" strip
- 3 diamonds of pineapple fabric
- 4 triangles of pineapple fabric

Assemble the top half of each block in two vertical rows as shown, using four half-diamonds, one half-triangle, one background diamond, and one background triangle.

Assemble the bottom half of each block in three diagonal rows as shown, using one half-triangle, three diamonds of pineapple fabric, four triangles of pineapple fabric, and one background triangle. Sew the top and bottom halves together to make a complete Pineapple block.

To assemble the quilt top:

3. Make three rows using two blocks in each row. Cut two background long diamonds from a 3¾" strip at 7" on the Clearview Triangle. (Long diamonds do have a reverse of their shape, so be sure to cut them in the correct direction.) Use the long diamonds as a setting strip between the blocks. End each row top and bottom with a 7½" background triangle half (cut a 4⅜" x 7½" rectangle and bisect it diagonally as shown). Add 7" setting strips between the rows. (Measure the height of the rows and adjust the setting strips accordingly.)

4. Add a 3¾" inner border of background fabric on all four sides. Then Terry added another border pieced from 4¼" triangles and flat pyramids cut from a 4" strip at 8" on the Clearview Triangle. End left and right borders with a 4¾" triangle half and top and bottom borders with a 4" x 6½" rectangle trimmed to a 60° angle. Add 7½" left and right final borders.

2 Vertical Rows
TOP HALF

3 Diagonal Rows
BOTTOM HALF

Complete Pineapple Block

Long Diamond

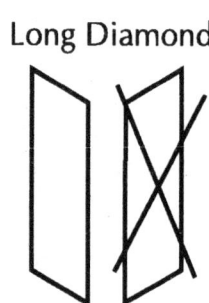

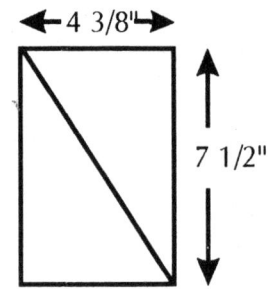

←— 4 3/8" —→

7 1/2"

Pineapple Quilt

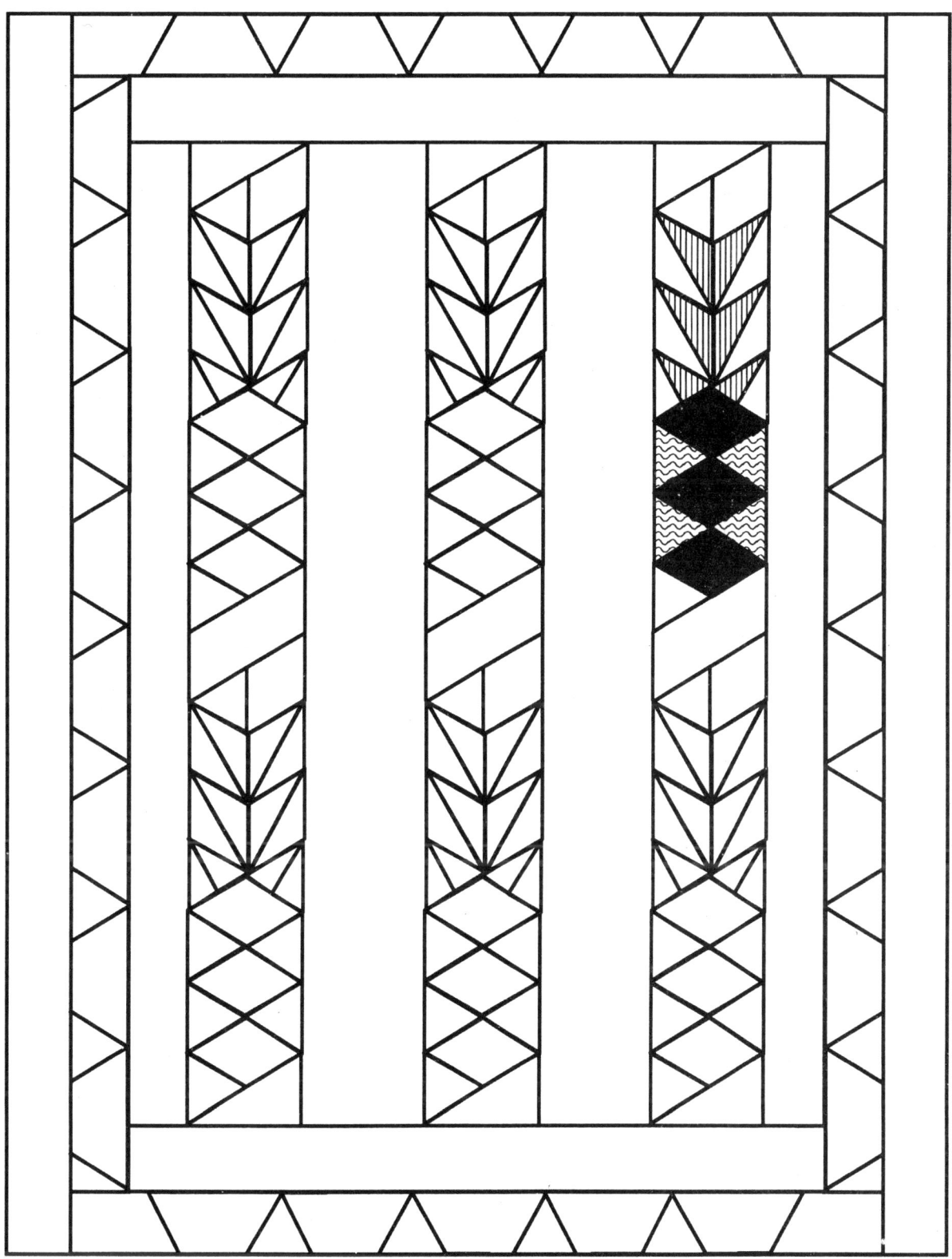

PINEAPPLE WALL HANGING
4" triangle size
Quilt with borders: 41¾" x 47½"

All fabric prewashed 42" wide.
Fabric requirements:
⅛ yd. dark green
1 yd. background fabric
¼ yd. pineapple fabrics

Directions:
Make three pineapple blocks as on pg. 20 and
assemble in one horizontal row, using 7½"
triangle halves at the top and bottom of each
block (cut as in the larger quilt), and 7"
background setting strips between the blocks.
Add a 3¾" inner border of background fabric,
and a 4½" final border.

Pineapple Wallhanging

MORNING GLORY

4" triangle size
Quilt with borders: 78" x 100½"

All fabric prewashed 45".
Fabric requirements:
7 yds. background fabric
⅔ yd. purple
½ yd. green
¼ yd. muslin

Directions:
1. Cut for one block:
- 2 background diamonds from a 7" strip (16 altogether)
- 2 background flat pyramids cut from a 3¾" strip at 7¼" on the Clearview Triangle (16 altogether)
- 6 background 4" triangles (48 altogether)
- 2 green and background half-diamonds from a 2⅜" set of strips (16 altogether)
- 2 green diamonds from a 3¾" strip (16 altogether)
- 6 half-triangles sandwich pieced from a muslin and purple 2⅝" set of strips (cut into 2⅝" x 4½" rectangles and then cut with Clearview Triangle) (48 altogether)
- 6 purple 4" triangles (48 altogether)

2. Sew the six half-triangles three and three, pressing as indicated. Then sew the two sets of three together across the center to make the flower twirl. Sew a purple 4" triangle to opposite sides of the twirl to make a flower diamond as shown at right.

3. From a green and background half-diamond, a background 4" triangle and a purple 4" triangle, make the larger triangle (A) as shown below. Make two of these. Sew on either side of the flower diamond as shown.

4. From a 4" purple triangle and a background flat pyramid make a larger triangle (B). Make two of these. From two background 4" triangles and a green 3¾" diamond make a larger triangle (C). Make two of these. Sew (B) and (C) onto a 7" background diamond as shown to make a strip as shown for the top and bottom of the block. Sew the flower strip and the two top and bottom strips together as shown to make one Morning Glory Block. Make eight complete blocks altogether.

Morning Glory Complete Block

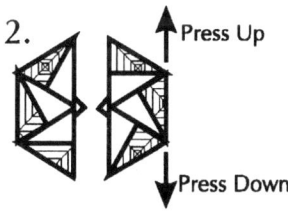

2. **Press Up** / **Press Down**

Flower Diamond
2.

Flower Strip
A

A

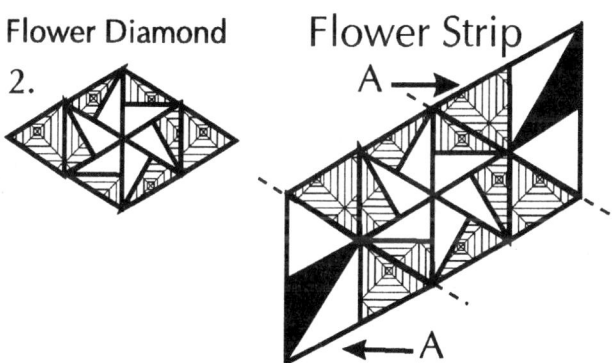

Top and Bottom Strip -Make Two of These
B →

← C

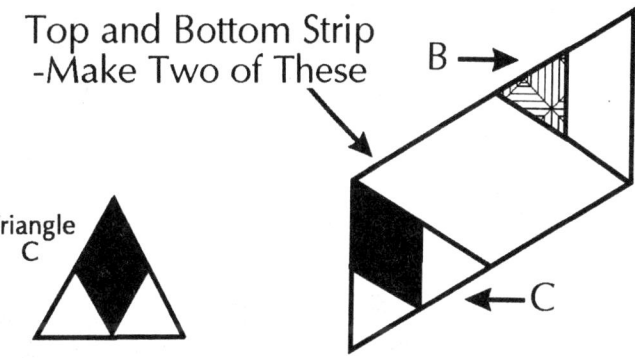

Triangle A

Triangle B

Triangle C

To assemble the quilt top:

5. The two outside rows are made from three blocks sewn together finished top and bottom with a 13½" x 10" background rectangle trimmed to a 60° angle with the Clearview Triangle as shown in the diagram. The center row is made from two blocks sewn together and finished top and bottom with a 13½" x 21¼" background rectangle trimmed to a 60° angle. All the rows should measure 78½".

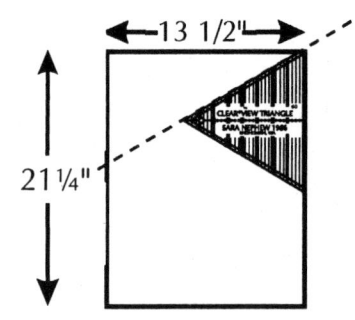

6. Sew the three rows together with 3¾" x 78½" background setting strip between. (Match centers and quarters and pin.) At left and right, add a 5½" x 78½" background setting strip to complete the quilt top. (Mark centers and quarters and pin.)

7. For the *Mock Scallop Border* cut:

- 24 background diamond halves cut from a 3¾" strip
- 20 background 4" triangles.
- 48 green diamond halves cut from a 2⅜" strip

Sew two green diamond halves to the background diamond half as shown. Make 24 of these mock scallops. Assemble the left and right border each from seven mock scallops and six background 4" triangles. Assemble the top and bottom border each from five mock scallops and four 4" background triangles. For a fancy corner, just match and pin centers and ends of the borders to the quilt top and seam on each side. For a square corner finish the ends of the left and right borders with a 4½" background triangle half cut from a 4½" triangle. Finish the ends of the top and bottom border with a 3¾" x 5¾" background rectangle trimmed to a 60° angle (and its reverse). Add a final 8" outside border.

Mock Scallop

Mock Scallop Border

Morning Glory

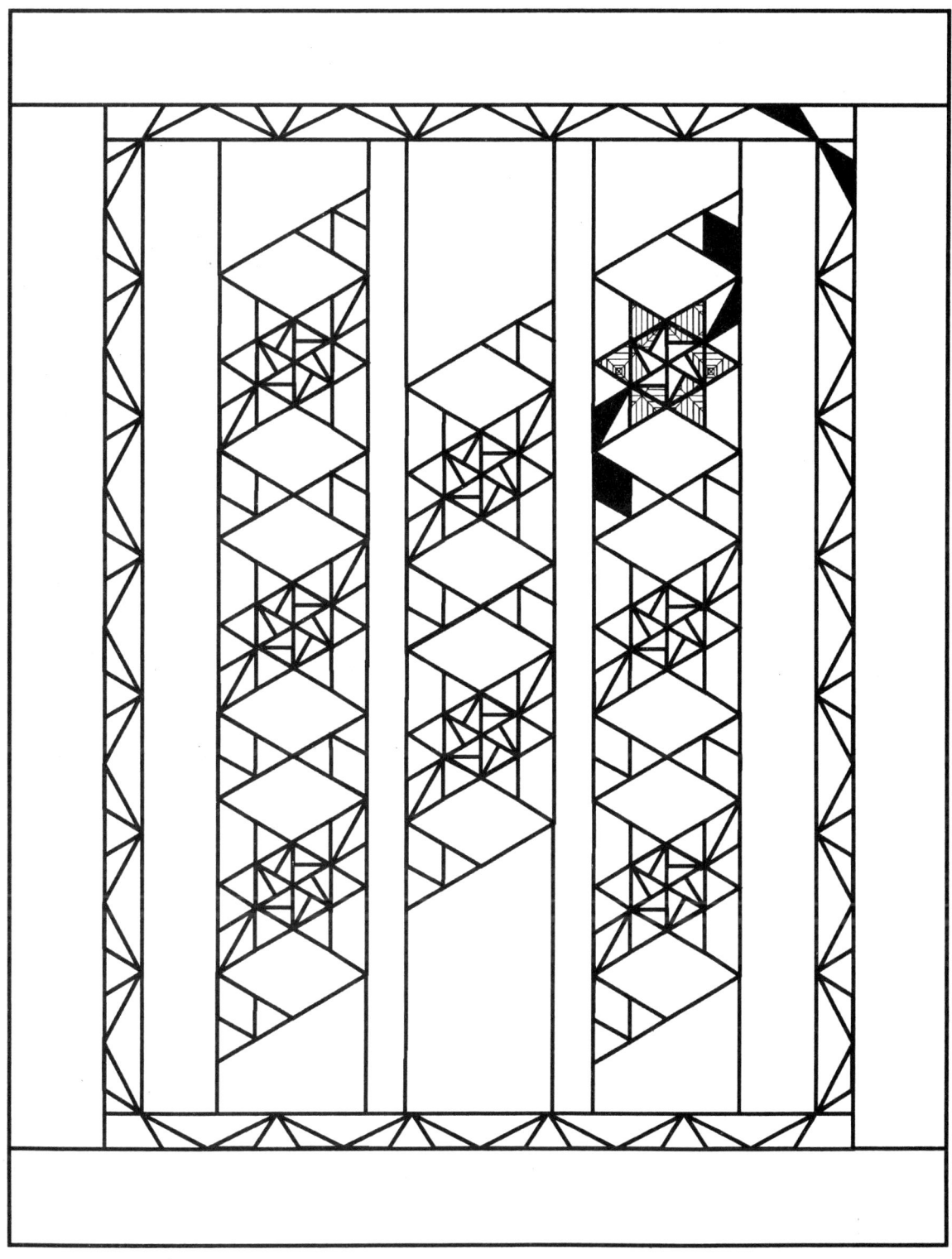

POISON IVY WALL HANGING

1½" triangle size
Quilt with borders: 16½" x 24¼"

All fabric prewashed 42" wide.
Fabric requirements:
¼ yd. leaf fabric
⅛ yd. stem fabric
¾ yd. background fabric

Directions:
1. Cut two 2½" strips of background fabric and one ¾" strip of stem fabric. Sew into a set of strips as shown. Cut flat pyramids from alternate sides of the set of strips at the 5¼" line on the Clearview Triangle. Then trim ½" off the top of the flat pyramid as shown so the finished stem section is 4¼" wide. Make nine of these.

2. Cut for each leaf section:
- 3 gem shapes from a 2" strip (cut 2" diamonds, then cut a 1" triangle off **one** end)
- 4 background 1½" triangles

Assemble according to the diagram. Make nine leaf sections. Sew the leaf and stem together for a complete *Poison Ivy* block. Make nine blocks.

3. To assemble the quilt top, cut:
- 6 background long diamonds from a 1¼" strip at 4¼" on the Clearview Triangle (long diamonds do have a reverse of their shape, so be sure you are cutting in the right direction)
- 6 background 5" triangle halves (cut 2⅞" x 5" rectangles and bisect as shown)

Sew the blocks into three vertical rows, with a background long diamond between the blocks, and a background triangle half at top and bottom. Measure the rows, then cut two 1¼" strips of background fabric the same length. Seam the rows together with these setting strips between the rows. Surround the quilt top with a 2" border of background fabric.

Long Diamond

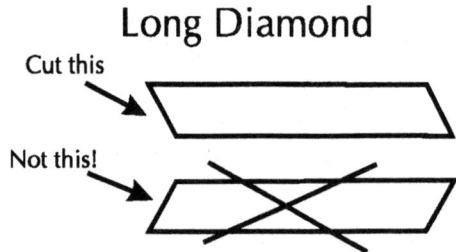

Cut this

Not this!

1. Set of Strips for Stem

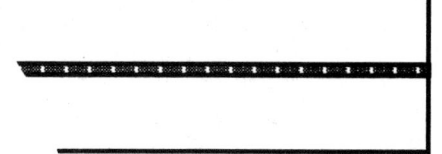

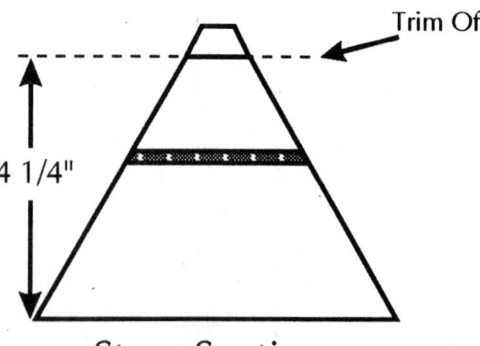

Trim Off

4 1/4"

Stem Section

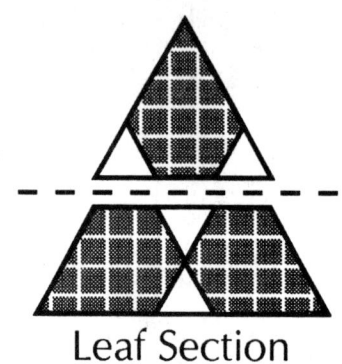

Leaf Section

Poison Ivy Block

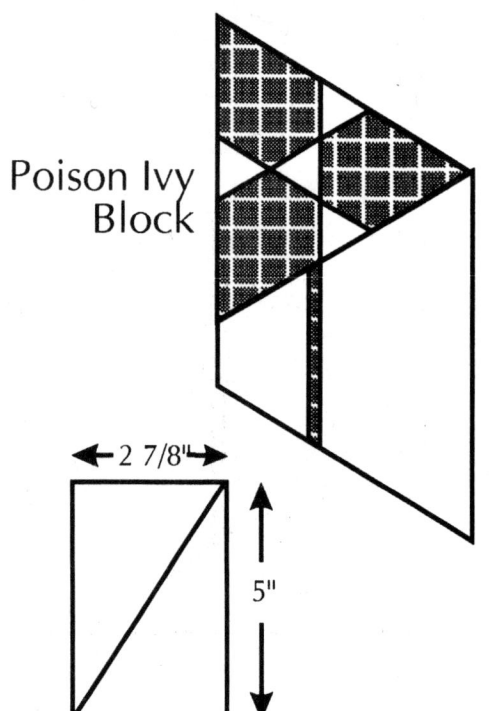

← 2 7/8" →

5"

Poison Ivy
Wall Hanging

POISON IVY QUILT

2½" triangle size
Quilt with borders: 62¾" x 86¼"

All fabric prewashed 42" wide.
Fabric requirements:
1 yds. leaf fabric
¼ yd. stem fabric
4½ yds. background fabric
1¼ yd. border fabric

Directions:
1. Cut two 5½" strips of background fabric and one 1" strip of stem fabric. Sew into a set of strips as shown. Cut flat pyramids from alternate sides of the set of strips at the 11¼" line on the Clearview Triangle. Then trim 2¼" off the top of the flat pyramid as shown so the finished stem section is 8¾" wide. Make 25 of these.

2. Cut for each leaf section:
• 3 gem shapes from a 4" strip (cut 4" diamonds, then cut a 2" triangle off **one** end)
• 4 background 2½" triangles

Assemble according to the diagram. Make 25 leaf sections. Sew the leaf and stem together for a complete *Poison Ivy* block. Make 25 blocks.

3. To assemble the quilt top, cut:
• 20 background long diamonds from a 2¼" strip at 9¼" on the Clearview Triangle (long diamonds do have a reverse of their shape, so be sure you are cutting in the right direction)
• 10 background 10" triangle halves (cut 5¾" x 10" rectangles and bisect as shown)

Sew the blocks into five vertical rows, with background long diamonds between the blocks, and a background triangle half at top and bottom. Measure the rows, then cut four 2¼" strips of background fabric the same length. Seam the rows together with these setting strips between the rows. Surround the quilt top with a 2¼" inner border of background fabric. Add a 4½" outer border.

Long Diamond

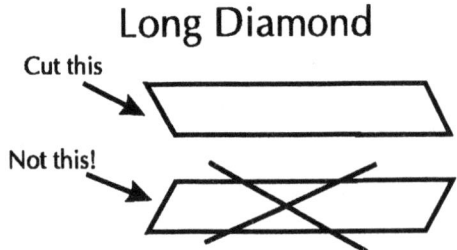

Cut this

Not this!

1. Set of Strips for Stem

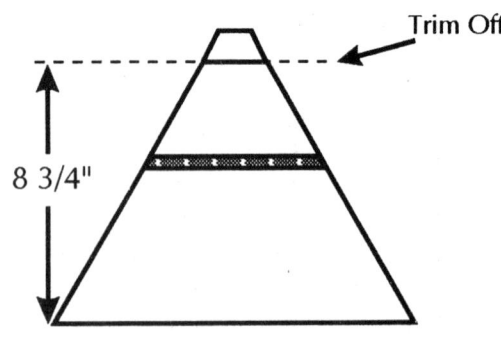

Trim Off

8 3/4"

Stem Section

Leaf Section

Poison Ivy Block

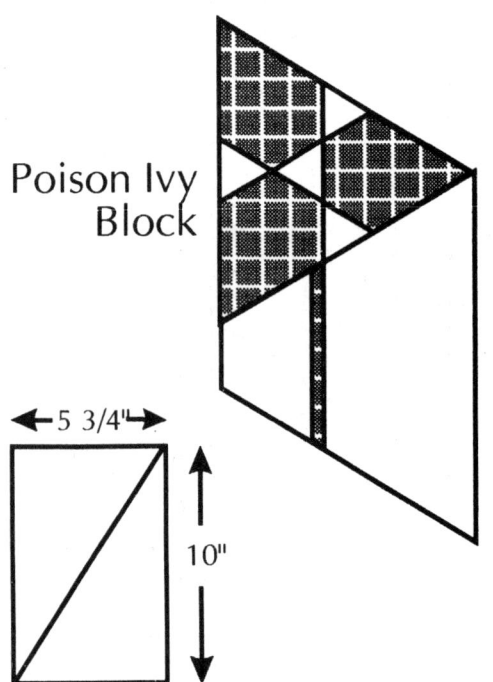

← 5 3/4" →

10"

Poison Ivy Quilt

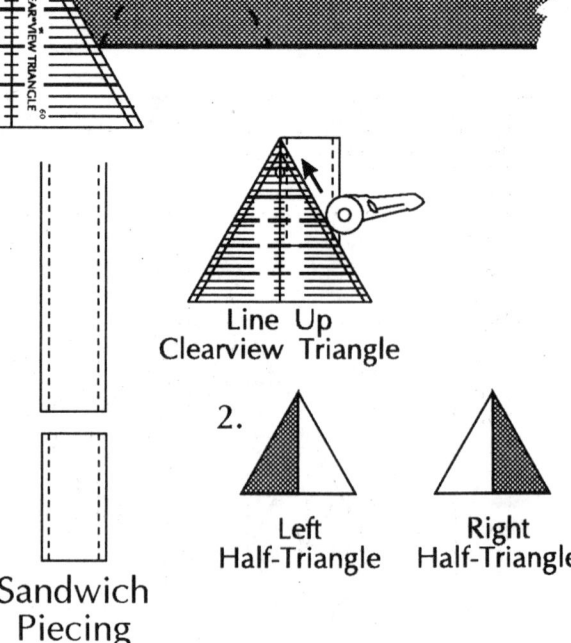

Cut 4" Triangles
From Iris Strips

1.

IRIS

4" triangle size
Quilt with borders: 80½" x 93¼"

All fabric prewashed 42" wide.
Fabric requirements:
7 yds. background fabric
¾ yds. leaf fabric
1 yd. light iris fabric (mixed)
1 yd. dark iris fabric (mixed)
¾ yd. dark border fabric

Directions:
1. Cut a 2¼" strip each of a light iris color and a dark iris color. Sew together lengthwise, pressing the seam to the dark. Cut 4" triangles from the set of strips. You will need three sets of strips and 48 triangles altogether.

2. From the background color and a matching iris color, sandwich piece half-triangles from a 2⅜" set of strips cut into rectangles 4½" high. You will need 48 left half-triangles and 48 right half-triangles.

3. Cut one 1" strip of leaf fabric and one 2¾" strip of background fabric. Make a set of strips as shown. Press to the dark. Cut into sections 4" high and sew the sections into one long strip. Center the Clearview Triangle on the green stem and cut 4" triangles from this strip. You will need 24 stem triangles altogether.

4. From leaf fabric and background fabric, sandwich piece 48 half-diamonds from a 2⅜" set of strips. Cut 72 background 4" triangles. Cut 24 background 7¼" triangles.

5. Assemble one Iris block from one background 7¼" triangle, three background 4" triangles, four half-triangles, two stripped triangles, one stem triangle, and two half-diamonds. Assemble in rows as shown in the diagram. Make 24 Iris blocks altogether.

Line Up
Clearview Triangle

2.

Left
Half-Triangle

Right
Half-Triangle

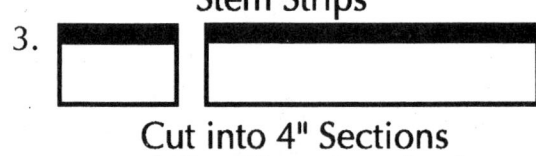

Sandwich
Piecing

Stem Strips

3.

Cut into 4" Sections
and Sew Together Again

Cut 4" Triangles from Strip
To Make Stem Triangle

5.

Piece
in
Rows

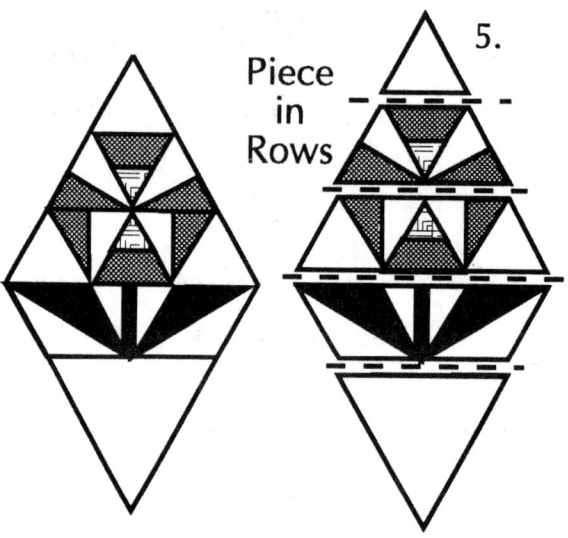

Half-Diamond

4.

Iris
Block

Iris

6. From background fabric cut:
- six 10½" triangles
- 4 diamond halves from a 6¼" strip
- 2 triangle halves from an 6⅜" x 11" rectangle, bisected diagonally as shown
- 2 triangle halves from a 11⅞" x 20¾" rectangle bisected diagonally as shown

7. Assemble the quilt top in diagonal rows according to the quilt diagram. Add a 3¾" strip of background fabric at the top and bottom, and then a 5¾" strip of background fabric at the left and right side.

To piece the *Ribbon* border:

8. Cut 72 background 4" triangles. Cut 38 left and 38 right long diamonds in a dark border color from a 2⅛" strip at 3¾" on the Clearview Triangle. (If you lay your strips right or wrong sides together, you will automatically cut left and right at the same time.) The left and right borders have 10 zigzags pointing in and the top and bottom have 9 zigzags pointing out. Finish both ends of each border with a background triangle half cut from a 4½" triangle.

OR: You can strip-piece part of this border if you wish. Cut two background 4" strips and one 2⅛" strip of dark iris color. Sew together into a set of strips as shown, pressing to the dark. Use the Clearview Triangle to cut a 60° angle at the end of the strip. Then cut off sections 3¾" wide, checking the 60° angle often. Finally cut a 3¾" triangle off each end of the section as shown. You will need 34 sections altogether. Cut 38 reverse long diamonds from the dark iris color from a 2⅛" strip at the 3¾" line on the Clearview Triangle. Sew together to make the border, adding background triangles as necessary. Then finish left and right border ends with a triangle half as above. Add a final 6" border of background fabric.

Diamond Half

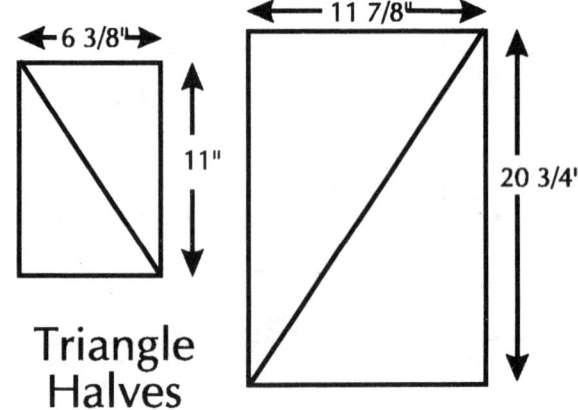

Triangle Halves

To Strip Piece Border
Cut 3 3/4" Sections

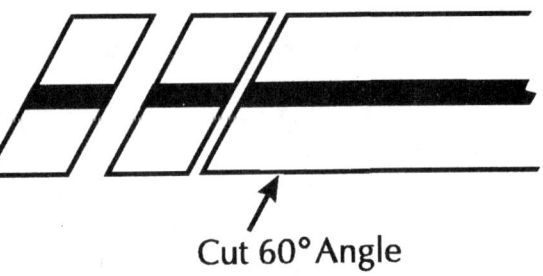

Cut 60° Angle

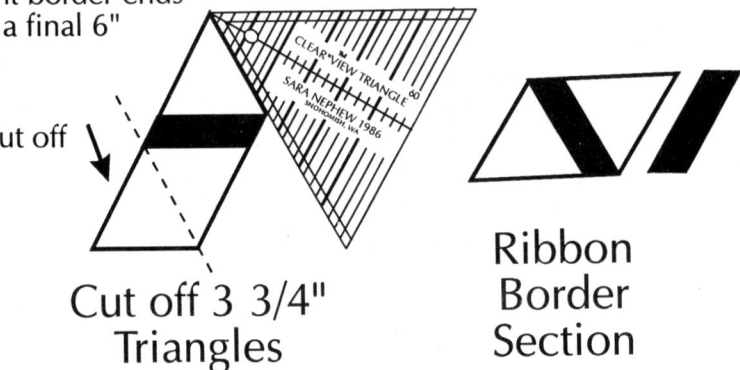

Cut off

Cut off 3 3/4"
Triangles

Ribbon
Border
Section

Pansy Garden, 65¾" x 79". A dusty peach background makes the pansy colors glow. Something different was tried in the colors of the little faces, giving them a checkerboard look. Pieced by Annette Austin. Hand quilted by Penny Wolf. (Right)

Pineapple Quilt, 60½" x 67½". This pineapple plantation flourishes in a big-print jungle. Volcanoes and lava add color to the background. Pieced and hand-quilted in an all-over meander by Terri Shinn. (Left)

Floral Wreath, 83" x 89½". Visual illusion forms a circle of flowers and buds in the center of this formal-looking quilt. The addition of a delicate border leaves lots of space for fine hand quilting. Or use a busy print for the background fabric and machine quilt to quickly have a finished project. Pieced by Kathleen Springer, machine quilted by Lynne Baxter. Details of leaves and flowers hand quilted by Connie Buss. (Right)

English Rose, 89" x 104½". A background fabric with a tea-dyed look, and darkened color choices like maroon add to the mellow antique look of this lacy design. Pieced by Diane Coombs and Sara Nephew. Hand quilted by Rose Herrera, Sara Nephew, and Lynn Williams. (Left)

Grapes, 79¼" x 91". Piecing this quilt reminded the author of stories of ladies quilting in a grape arbor. Careful piecing places a little star in each bunch of grapes. Hand quilted by Nadine Darby. (Right page)

English Rose with Wild Rose Border, 55¼" x 62¾", is a wonderful quilt to take a nap under when you've finished working in your garden. The background is filled with beautiful feather quilting. Hand quilted by Penny Wolf. (Top Left)

Poison Ivy Wall Hanging, 16½" x 24¼". Although one might prefer not to get too close to the actual plant, the idea of "poison" might be an inspiration for a color scheme. Pieced and hand quilted by Lynne Williams. (Top Right)

Shamrock, 61" x 75". A mix of thirties' reprint fabrics spreads sunshine over these leaves. The closely quilted grid is also typical of depression-era quilts, though this is a modern piece. Pieced and hand quilted by Terri Shinn. (Left)

Positively Pansy, 84" x 92¾". Dainty pansy faces arrange themselves as in a formal garden. A special scallop border makes a fence. Pick bright pinks, rich purples, and other striking pansy colors for this stunning quilt. Hand quilted by Penny Wolf.

Baby Rose, 35" x 35¼". Reducing these motifs to an almost miniature size makes them even more appealing. A delicate yet striking baby quilt or Christmas wall hanging. Hand quilted by Penny Wolf. (Right)

Cherries, 60" x 66". Two different black fabrics and a simple border combine with the cherry motif for a folk art look. A design of twining branches and cherry leaves was drawn freehand and beautifully hand quilted in red. Quilted by Nadine Darby. (Bottom)

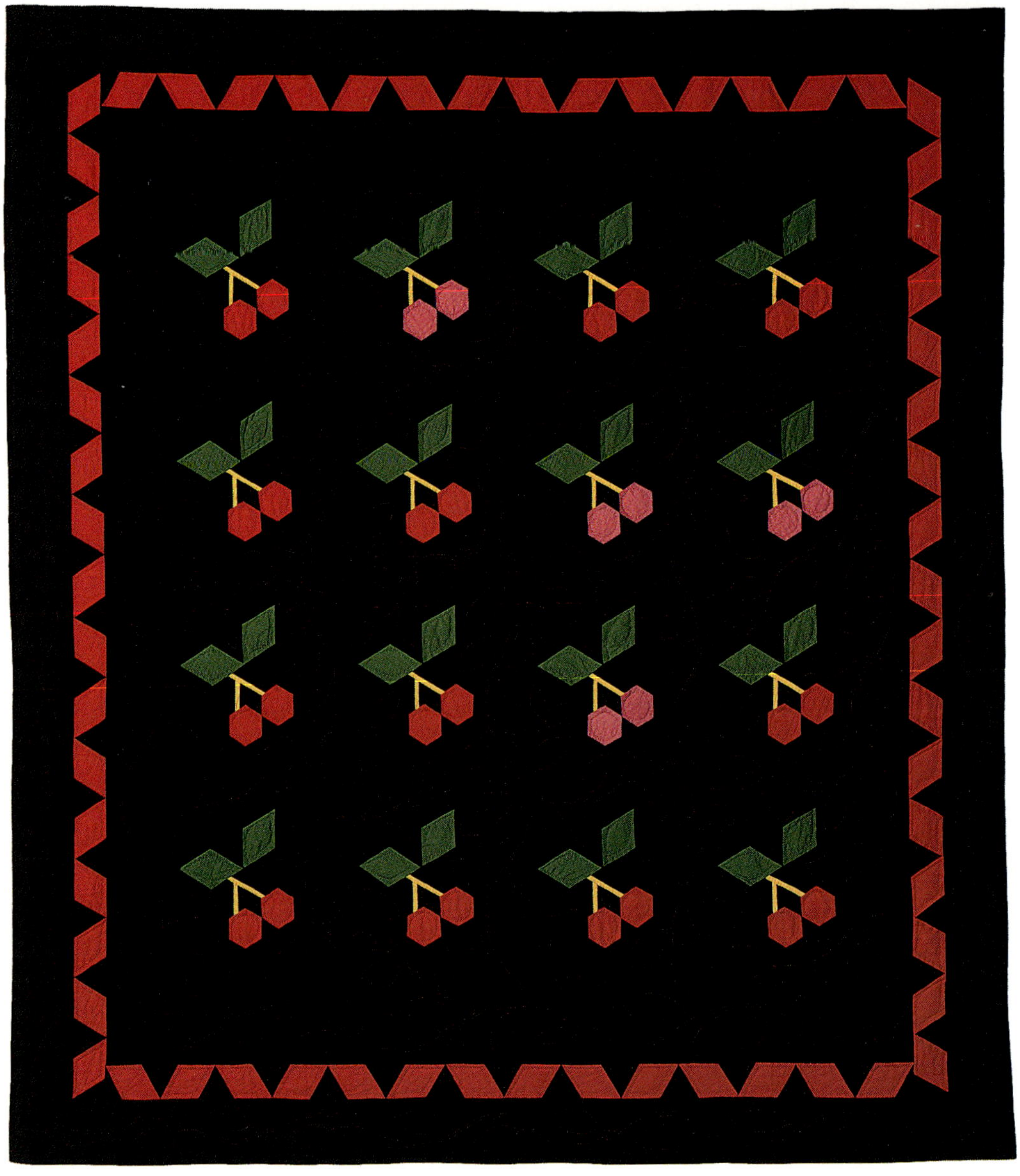

Mixed Fruit, 58½" x 69½". A warm day on an flourishing homestead is called to mind by the sunlight-filled background fabric. Cherry and grape leaves mix around the border. Hang this quilt near a table laden with delicious food to dress up any event. Machine quilted by Lynne Baxter, and the details of fruit and leaves hand quilted by Sara Nephew. (Left)

Morning Glory, 78" x 100½". These happy flowers twirl and dance across the surface of their quilt. A simple pieced border frames the design, while a busy print background calls for machine quilting and a quick finish. Pieced by Joan Dawson. Machine quilted by Lynne Baxter, with floral details hand quilted by Joan. (Right)

Poison Ivy Quilt, 62¾" x 86¼". Annette prefers to call this quilt Twining Ivy, and made it as a gift for her husband. The mix of green fabrics against a tea-colored background is natural looking and very masculine. Pieced and hand quilted by Annette Austin. (Top Left)

Pineapple Wall Hanging, 41¾" x 47½". Have you been to Hawaii? Ripe pineapple with golden fruit and dark green leaves are silhouetted against a clear blue sky. Pieced by Mary Pierce. (Top Right)

Iris, 80½" x 93¼". Iris faces in many realistic colors are surrounded by a purple ribbon. Strip and sandwich piecing can help to make this a relatively quick project. The use of black or muslin background fabric would also be very striking. (Left)

CHERRIES

1¾" triangle size
Quilt with borders: 60" x 66"

All fabric prewashed 42" wide.
Fabric requirements:
4½ yds. background fabric
½ yd. leaf fabric
¾ yd. cherry fabric
⅛ yd. stem fabric

Directions: First strip-piece four parts of the block:

Stem Triangle A

1. Cut a ⅞" strip of background fabric, a 2⅛" strip of background fabric, and a ¾" strip of stem fabric. Sew into a set of strips as shown. Press to the dark if possible. Cut 2¾" triangles as shown from the set of strips. Discard the triangles from the opposite side. You will need 16 of Stem Triangle A.

Stem Section B

2. Cut a ¾" strip of stem fabric and a 1¼" strip of background fabric. Sew into a set of strips. Cut long diamonds from the set of strips as shown, at the 2½" line on the Clearview Triangle. You will need 16 of Stem Section B.

Leaf Section C

3. Cut two background 2¾" strips and one 2½" strip of the leaf color. Sew together into a set of strips as shown, pressing to the dark. Begin by cutting a 60° angle at the end of the strip. Then cut off sections 2½" wide, checking the 60° angle often. Finally cut a 2½" triangle off each end of the section as shown. You will need 16 sections altogether.
Or: Cut 16 diamonds from a 2½" strip of the leaf color and 32 background 2¾" triangles . Sew into 16 of Leaf Pair C.

Leaf Section D

4. Cut one background 1½" strip and one 2½" strip of the leaf color. Sew together into a set of strips as shown, pressing to the dark. Begin by cutting a 60° angle at the end of the strip. Then cut off sections 2½" wide, checking the 60° angle often. You will need 16 of section D altogether.

Stem Triangle A

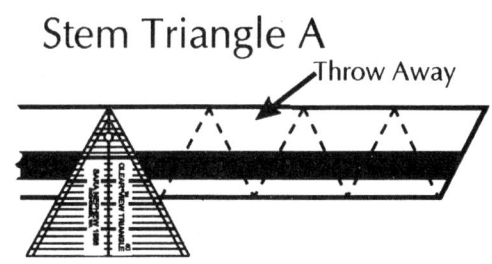

Throw Away

Stem Section B

Leaf Section C

Cut 60° Angle

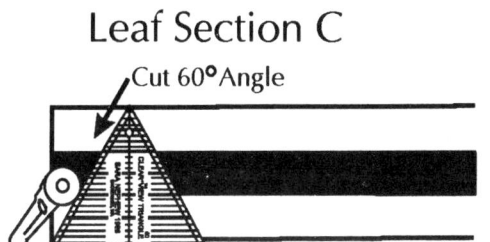

Cut 2 1/2" Sections

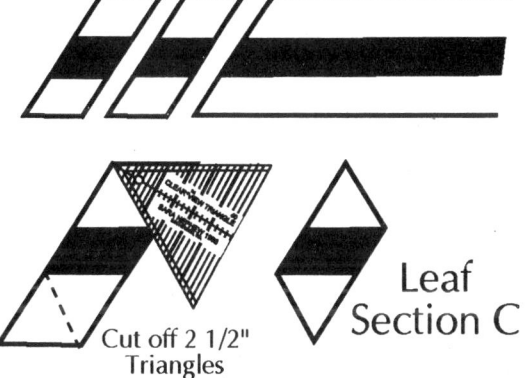

Cut off 2 1/2" Triangles

Leaf Section C

Leaf Section D

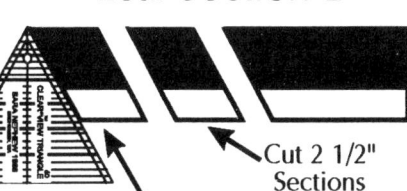

Cut 2 1/2" Sections

Trim to 60° Angle

5. Cut these additional pieces for each block:
- 2 red hexagons from a 2½" strip (cut 2½" diamonds, then cut a 1¼" triangle off each end)
- 2 background 1¾" triangles
- 2 background 3¾" triangles
- 1 background 4¾" triangle

Assemble the block according to the piecing diagram. Make 16 *Cherries* blocks.
TIP *After sewing the leaf sections together grade out a wedge of the excess seam allowance to reduce bulk. (See diagrams on pg.71.)*

To assemble the quilt:
6. Cut:
- 8 background 8¼" triangle halves (cut four rectangles 4¾" x 8¼" and bisect as shown)
- 12 background long diamonds from a 4½" strip cut at 7½" on the Clearview Triangle

Make four rows of blocks, using the long diamonds as setting strips between the blocks, and finishing the rows top and bottom with the triangle halves. Measure the length of the rows. (Should be 46".)

7. Cut 4½" strips of background fabric for setting strips between the rows. Piece them to the same length as the rows of blocks. Sew the strips and the rows together as in the quilt diagram. Add a 5" border of background fabric.

Piece the *Cherry Leaf* border:
8. Make 32 of Leaf Pair C as in #3 above. Cut 32 diamonds in the border diamond color from a 2½" strip. Sew together to make the borders. The left and right borders have eight and a half leaf pairs and the top and bottom have seven leaf pairs. Finish both ends of each border with a background triangle half cut from a 3¼" triangle.

OR: Cut 64 background 2¾" triangles. Cut 64 diamonds of the border color from a 2½" strip. Sew together to make the borders, finishing left and right border ends as above.

Add a final 4" border of background fabric.

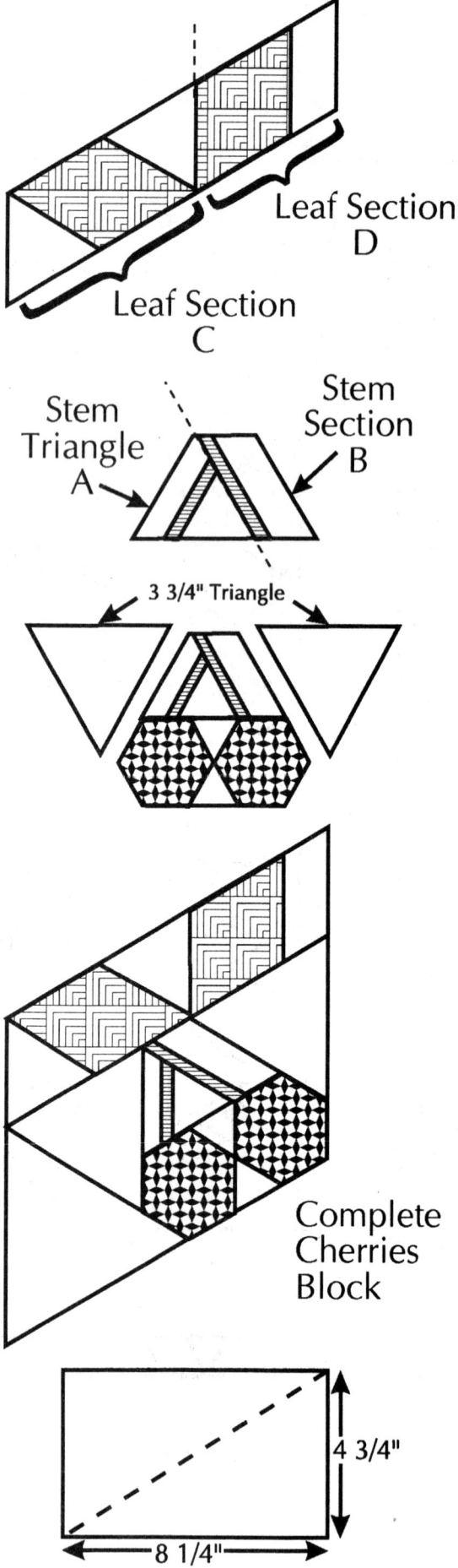

Leaf Section D

Leaf Section C

Stem Triangle A

Stem Section B

3 3/4" Triangle

Complete Cherries Block

4 3/4"

8 1/4"

Cherries

FLORAL WREATH

3" triangle size
Quilt with borders: 83" x 89½"

All fabric prewashed 42" wide.
Fabric requirements:
½ yd. flower fabric
1 yd. green fabric
6¾ yds. background fabric

Directions:
1. Cut :
- 6 green diamonds from a 2¾" strip
- 12 diamonds of background fabric from a 2¾" strip
- 6 background 3" triangles (30 will be needed altogether, cut as necessary)
- 1 background 7½" triangle

Sew one green diamond, one background diamond, and one background triangle into strip A as shown. Make three strips and three strips reversed. Sew three of strip A reversed onto the 7½" triangle to make the center hexagon.

2. Sandwich piece 66 half-diamonds from 1⅞" strips of green and background fabrics. (You will need five or six sets of strips altogether.) Cut 18 flower fabric 3" triangles. From a half-diamond, a 3" flower fabric triangle, and a 3" background triangle, make a larger pieced triangle as shown. Make three of these. Sew onto the center hexagon to make a larger center triangle for the medallion.

3. Sandwich piece 18 half-triangles from 2" strips of flower and background fabric. Sew the half-triangles into six sets of three, pressing as indicated. Then sew two sets of three together across the center to make the flower twirl. Make three flower twirls altogether. Sew a flower 3" triangle to opposite sides of the twirl to make a flower diamond as shown at right/left.

4. From a half-diamond, a background triangle, and a flower fabric triangle, construct strip B. Sew to the flower diamond as shown. From two background diamonds and a 3" flower fabric triangle make strip C. Sew this strip to the previous unit as shown to make a gem shape.

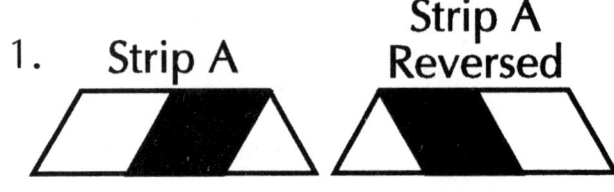

1. Strip A — Strip A Reversed

Center Hexagon

Pieced Triangle

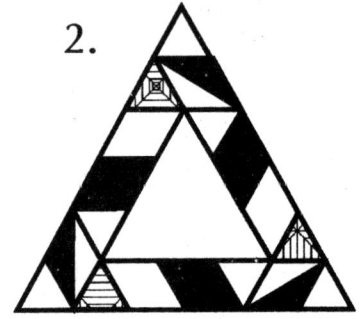

2.

Larger Center Triangle

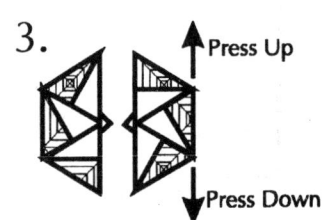

3. Press Up — Press Down

Flower Twirl

Flower Diamond

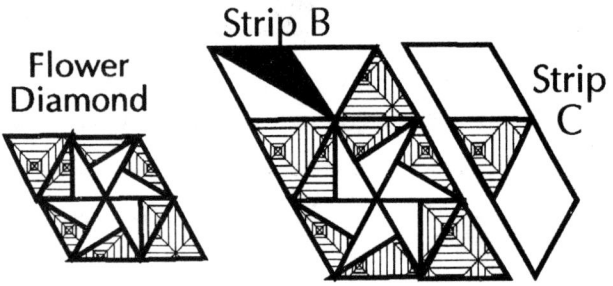

Strip B

Strip C

Floral Wreath

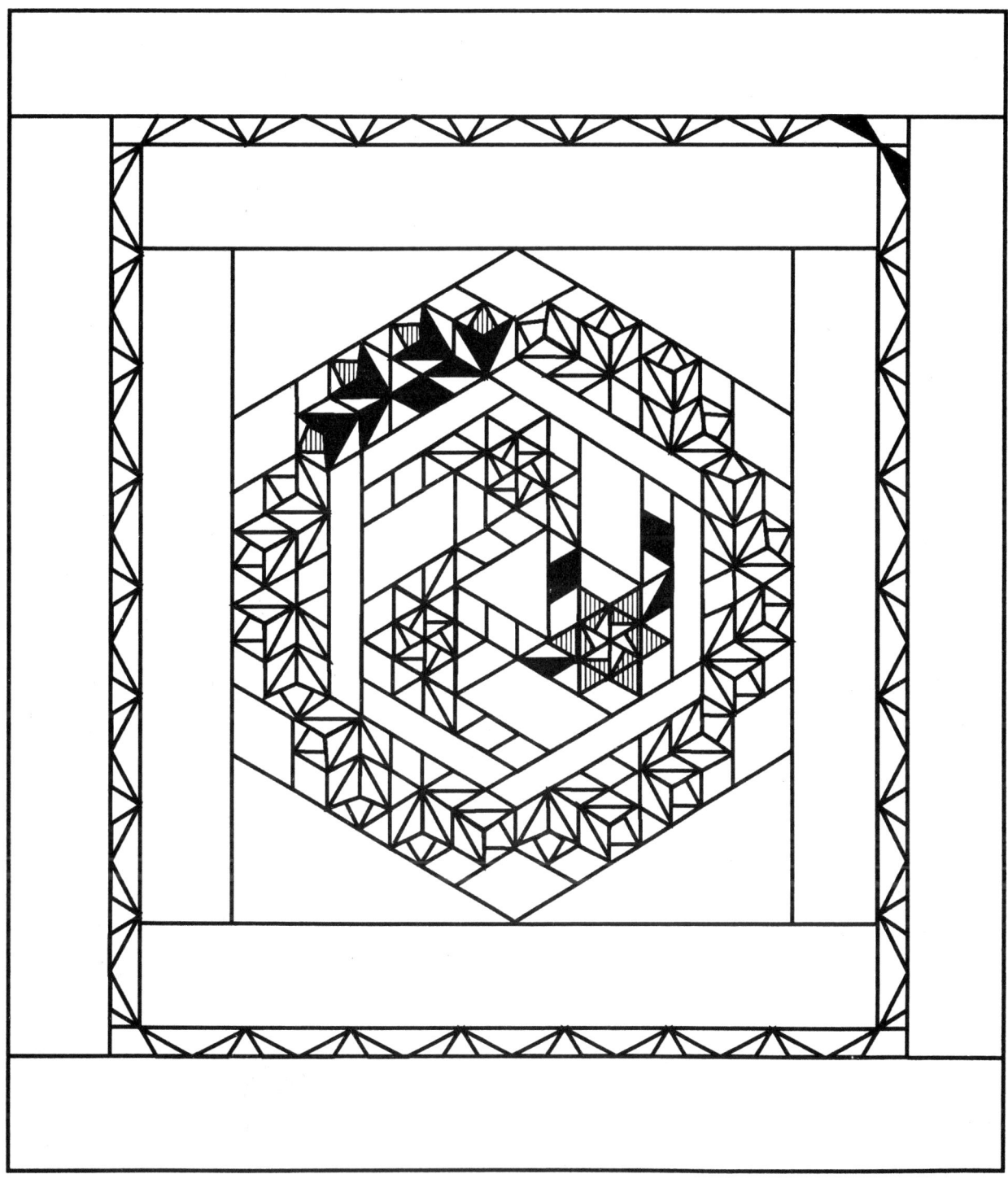

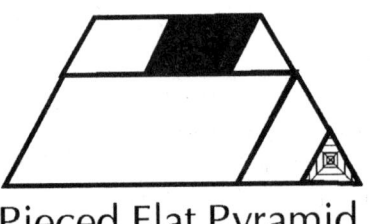

Pieced Flat Pyramid

5. Cut from background fabric:
- 3 flat pyramids from a 2¾" strip at the 5¼" line on the Clearview Triangle
- 3 long diamonds from a 5" strip at the 7¼" line on the Clearview Triangle

Use the above pieces, plus the remaining strips A and the remaining 3" flower fabric triangles, to make three large pieced flat pyramids. Sew these to the gem shape from #4 as shown to make the three side sections to be sewn onto the center triangle from #3.

5.

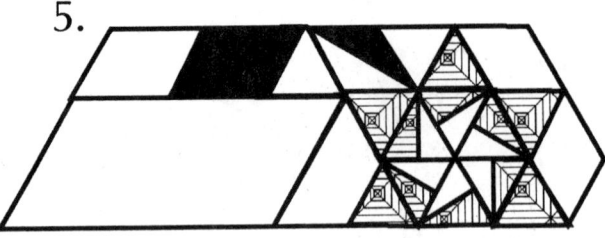

Side Section

6. Sew one side section to the center triangle, sewing from the right edge towards the left. Sew to about the center of the last background triangle on the left side and leave the remaining inch or so unsewn for now. Going in a clockwise direction, sew the next side section on completely. Then sew the third side section on completely. Finally, finish the seam of the first side section. This completes the center of the floral medallion.

6.

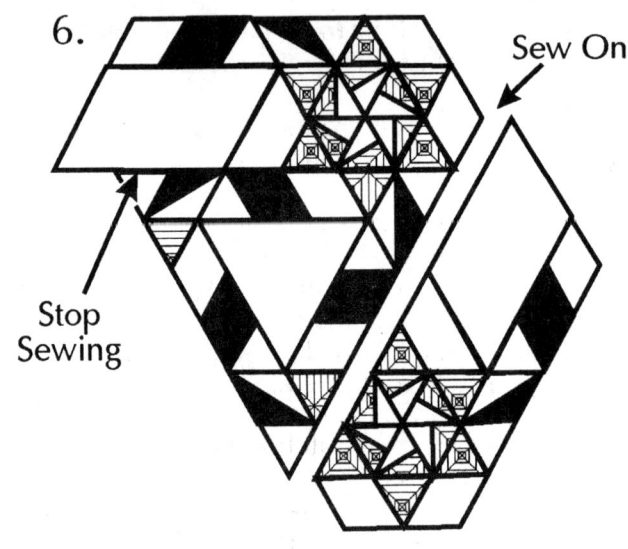

Sew On

Stop Sewing

7. Cut a strip of background fabric 2¾" wide, and sew it onto one side of the medallion, trimming it even with the adjacent sides. Do this on three separate sides of the medallion. Cut additional strips as needed. Then sew the strip(s) onto the remaining three sides, trimming even with the edges again.

8. Cut and piece 24 teardrop units (cut teardrops from a 3⅜" strip and triangle halves from a 3½" strip). From a 2¾" green diamond and two background 3" triangles, make a pieced triangle as shown. Make five more of these.

9. From four half-diamonds, a background diamond, and a teardrop unit, Assemble a *Wild Rose* border unit in rows. (see diagram on next page) Sew together according to the diagram, sewing from the edge of each point to the inside seam allowance and backstitching. Set in a teardrop unit and a half-diamond as shown. This completes one border unit. Make 12 border units altogether. Seam two border units, a pieced triangle and a 3" background triangle into a border section as shown. Make six of these altogether. Sew the border sections onto the six sides of the medallion, sewing only from seam allowance to seam allowance and backstitching.

6.

Finish Sewing Seam

8.

10. Also sew the six short sides seams only from seam allowance to seam allowance and backstitch at each end. Cut six background 5" diamonds. Set these diamonds into the six angles around the *Wild Rose* border. This completes the floral wreath.

To assemble the quilt top:
11. Cut two rectangles of background fabric 12" x 21¼". Bisect one rectangle diagonally as shown, and the other on the reverse diagonal. Sew the resulting triangle halves at the top and bottom of the floral wreath to make the quilt into a rectangle. Add 8¾" borders of background fabric at the left and right. (Measure the height of the quilt and cut the borders to this length. Match centers and quarters and pin.) Add 10¾" borders of background fabric top and bottom.

12. For the **Mock Scallop Border** cut:
- 30 background diamond halves cut from a 2⅞" strip
- 26 background 3" triangles.
- 60 green diamond halves cut from a 1⅞" strip

Sew two green diamond halves to the background diamond half as shown. Make 30 of these mock scallops. Assemble the left and right border each from eight mock scallops and seven background 3" triangles. Assemble the top and bottom border each from seven mock scallops and six 3" background triangles. For a fancy corner, just match and pin centers and ends of the borders to the quilt top and seam on each side. For a square corner finish the ends of the left and right borders with a 3½" background triangle half cut from a 3½" triangle. Finish the ends of the top and bottom border with a 2¾" x 4⅜" background rectangle trimmed to a 60° angle (and its reverse).

13. Add a final 10½" outer border of background fabric.

9.

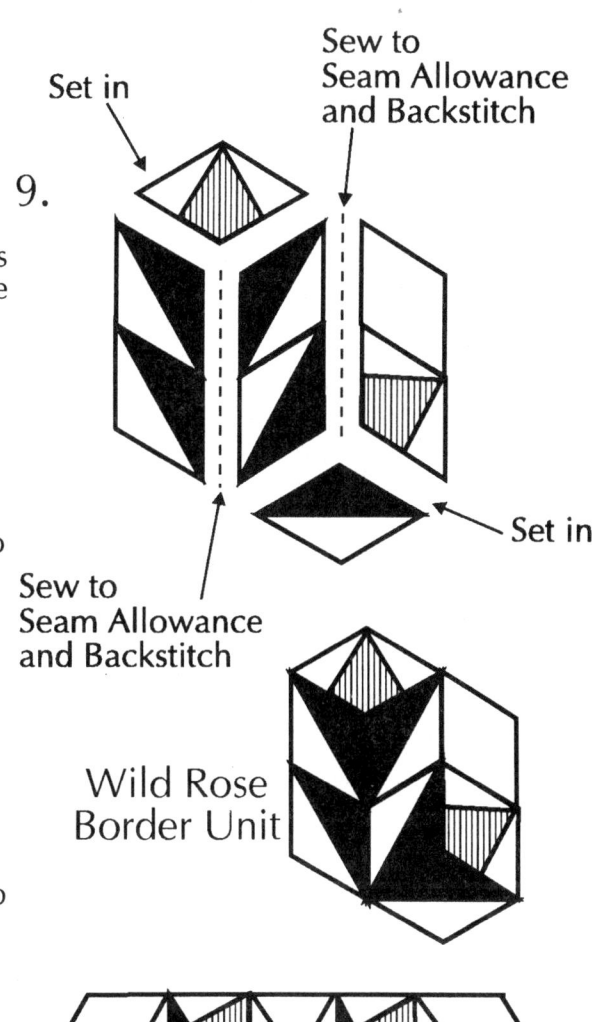

Set in

Sew to Seam Allowance and Backstitch

Sew to Seam Allowance and Backstitch

Set in

Wild Rose Border Unit

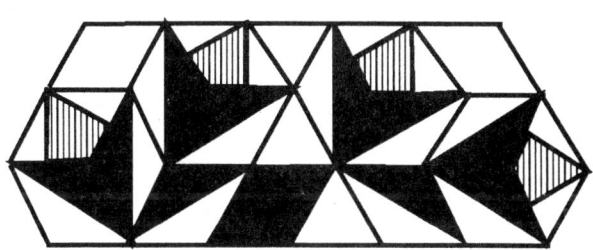

Wild Rose Border Section

Mock Scallop

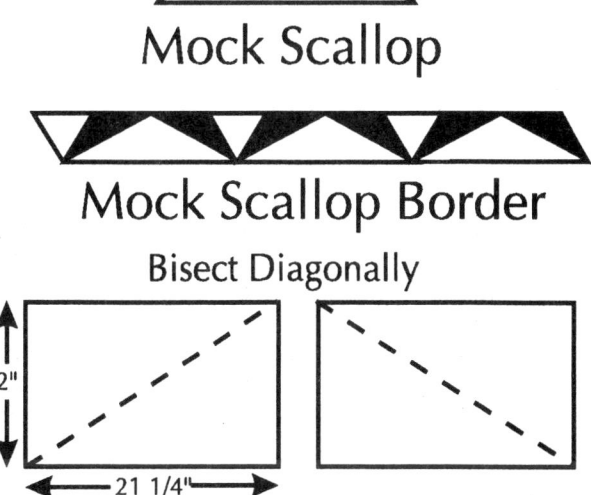

Mock Scallop Border

Bisect Diagonally

4 3/4"

2 3/4"

12"

21 1/4"

 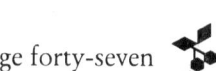

ENGLISH ROSE
4" triangle size

Quilt with borders: 89" x 104½"

All fabric prewashed 42" wide.
Fabric requirements:
½ yd. gold fabric
¾ yd. mauve fabric
1½ yds. burgundy fabric
3 yds. dark green fabric
6½ yds. tan fabric

Directions:

1. To piece one block of ENGLISH ROSE: Sandwich-piece six half-triangles from 2⅜" strips of gold and mauve. Assemble a center twirl from two groups of three as shown. Seam mauve triangles to three separate sides of the twirl. This is the center triangle of the block.

2. Make six teardrop units as shown from tan and burgundy. Seam two teardrop units and a mauve triangle into a strip as shown. Make two more of these. Sew the strip onto three sides of the center triangle to make a hexagon.

3. From six green diamonds and 12 tan triangles make pieced triangles (A) as shown. (48 needed altogether) Sew three of these pieced triangles on three separate sides of the center hexagon.

4. Make six teardrop units as shown from tan and burgundy. Cut 12 green diamond halves from 2⅜" strips. Cut 12 triangle halves from 7¾" tan triangles. (six left and six right) Sew a diamond half to each triangle half as shown. Press to the triangle half. Then sew the diamond halves green sides together according to the diagram. Sew from the edge to inside seam allowance, stop and backstitch. Set in a teardrop unit. Make five more of these Rosebuds. (B) (50 needed altogether)

5. From one pieced triangle (A) and two Rosebuds (B) piece a strip (C) as shown. Make two more of these. Sew strip (C) on three sides of the triangle resulting from #3. Pin to match points. *This completes one block. Five complete blocks will be needed.*

Center Twirl

Center Triangle

1.

2.

Teardrop Unit

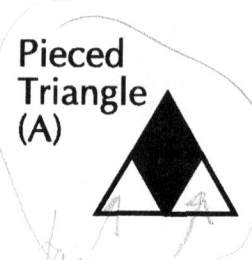

Pieced Triangle (A)

3.

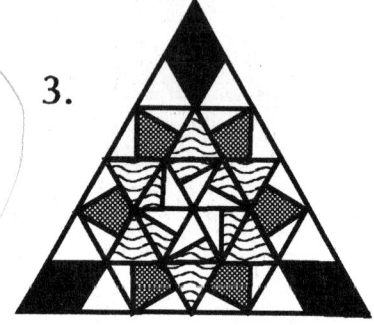

4.

Stop and Backstitch

Set in Teardrop Unit

Rosebud(B)

5.

English Rose Block

Strip (C)

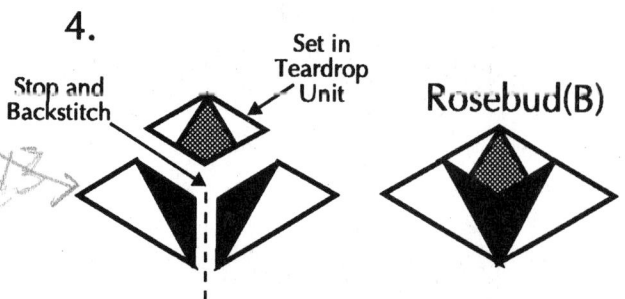

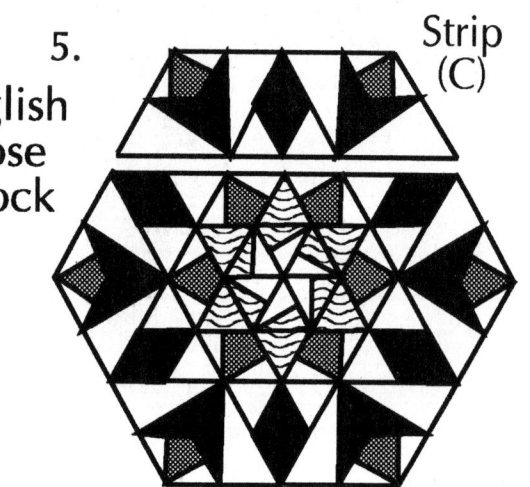

English Rose

6. To piece a half-block: make four gold and mauve half-triangles as above. Sew two half-triangles together as shown. Cut a gold 2⅝" x 4½" rectangle and bisect it as shown to produce triangle halves. Cut two mauve diamond halves from a 2⅜" strip. Sew the gold triangle half, the mauve diamond half, and a 4" mauve triangle to the pair of half triangles as shown to make a pieced triangle half. Make another one of these.

7. Sew a teardrop unit and a mauve 4½" triangle half onto the left side as shown. Seam two teardrop units and a mauve triangle into a strip. Sew onto the pieced triangle half as shown. Then on the left and right add a tan triangle and a green diamond half cut from a 2⅜" strip to produce a pieced diamond half.

8. Sew together a pieced triangle (A) and a Rosebud (B) and sew this onto the left side of the pieced diamond half. Finally add a strip (C) to complete the half-block. Make two half-blocks.

9. Cut:
- 8 tan 13¾" triangles
- 8 tan 14¼" triangle halves cut from 14¼" triangles

Sew three rows of blocks and half-blocks according to the quilt diagram. Sew the rows together. Add a 3¾" top and bottom, and a 4½" left and right, inner border of tan fabric.

SETTING IN A TEARDROP
1. Right sides together, sew the teardrop unit to one inside edge of a seamed pair of diamond halves. Sew only up to the inside seam allowance and backstitch. Remove from under presser foot.

2. Line up the two remaining raw edges. Begin at the inside seam allowance, take a backstitch and seam to the outside edge.

Pair of
Half-Triangles

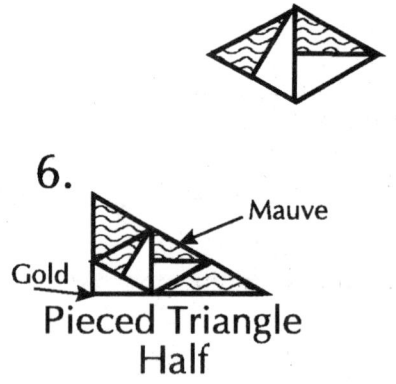

6.

Gold — Mauve

Pieced Triangle
Half

To get
two identical
triangle halves

Gold

4 1/2"

← 2 5/8" →

7.

Pieced Diamond Half

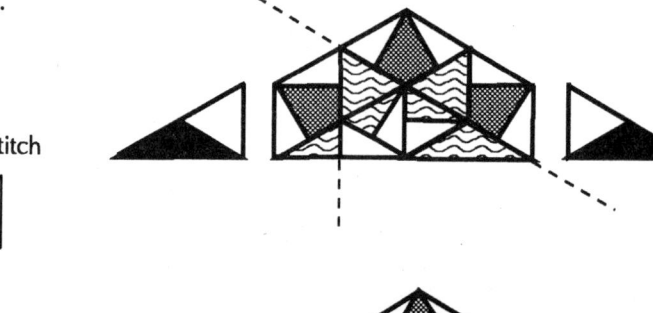

1. Stop and backstitch

2. Backstitch again

English Rose Half-Block

To piece two borders:

10. Sandwich-piece 4" tan and green matched triangles and sew them together to make a *Silhouette* border. Use 21 matching triangles on the left and right side and 18 on the top and bottom. Add a tan triangle on the green end. Then finish both ends of all four borders with a 4½" green triangle half cut from a 4½" triangle.

11. For each strip D, cut:
- 2 tan 7¾" tan triangle halves cut from a 7¾" triangle
- 2 teardrop units pieced with quarter hexes as shown from a 3¾" strip (left and right)
- 2 sandwich pieced green and tan half-diamonds from 2⅜" strips (press to background)
- 2 green diamond halves from a 2⅜" strip
- 1 pieced triangle (A)

Assemble left and right Rosebuds, setting in the teardrop units as shown. Add a pieced triangle (A) to complete Strip (D). Then assemble *English Rose* borders from Strips (C) and (D), Finish the ends of the top and bottom borders by sewing on a 4½" background triangle half as shown and then trimming the excess point even with the triangle half. Finish the ends of the left and right rows with a 6¾" x 7" rectangle trimmed to a 60° angle.

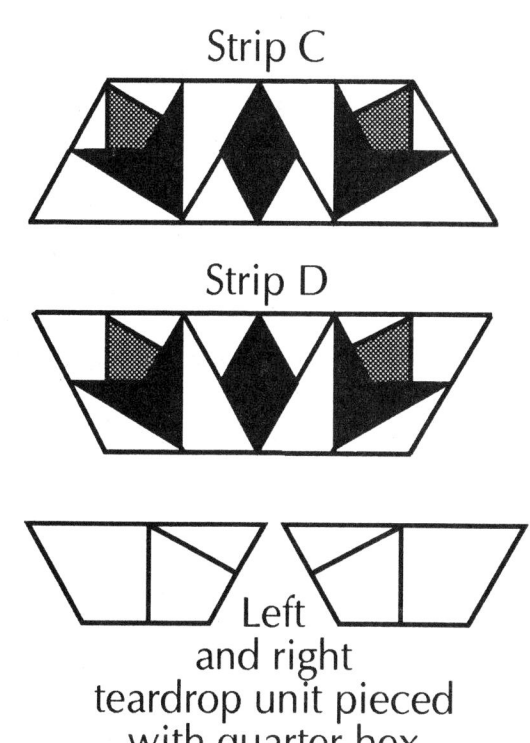

Strip C

Strip D

Left and right teardrop unit pieced with quarter hex

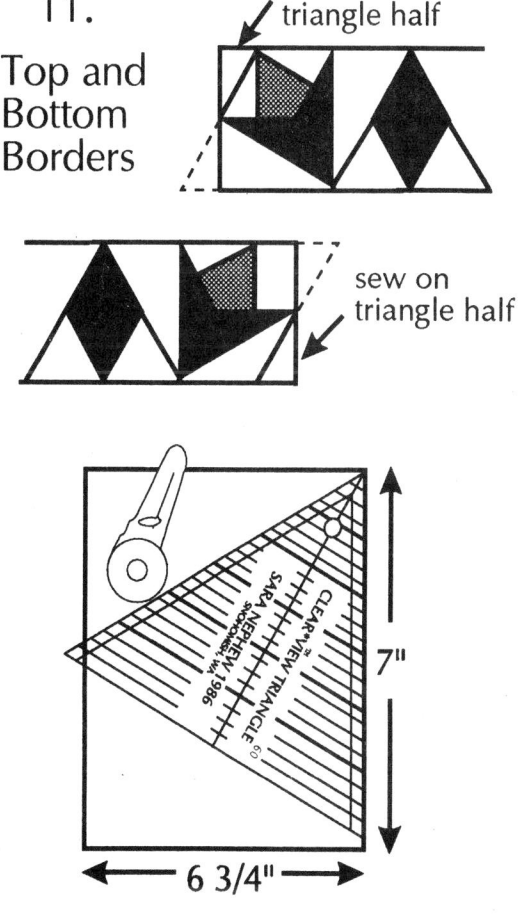

11.

Top and Bottom Borders

sew on triangle half

sew on triangle half

7"

6 3/4"

ENGLISH ROSE..with WILD ROSE border

3" triangle size
Quilt with borders: 55¼" x 62¾"
All fabric prewashed 42" wide.

Fabric requirements:
¼ yd. pink fabric
½ yd. light red fabric
¼ yd. maroon fabric
¾ yd. green fabric
3¾ yds. white-on-white muslin

Directions:
1. Cut for one block of ENGLISH ROSE:
- 6 sandwich pieced half-triangles from red and pink 2" strips
- 6 red triangles.
- 6 maroon teardrops (3⅜" strip) and 12 muslin triangle halves (3½" strip) for six teardrop   units
- 6 green diamonds
- 12 muslin triangles
- 6 teardrop units from red and muslin
- 12 green diamond halves (1⅞" strip)
- 12 muslin triangle halves from 5¾" triangles

Assemble one *English Rose* block according to the diagrams on pg.48.

2. To frame and float the block: cut two 9¾" muslin triangles. Sew onto opposite sides of the block. Cut two 30° muslin triangles measuring 21" on the long side. Sew to the medallion as shown. (This will not reach completely to the end of the 9¾" triangles. Trim the points of the 9¾" triangles even with the edges of the 30° triangles.) Add a 5" strip of muslin to each side of the center panel.

To piece the WILD ROSE border:
3. (28 red or maroon teardrop units and 70 green and white sandwich pieced half-diamonds will be needed.) From four green and white half-diamonds, a muslin diamond, and a teardrop unit, assemble three rows as shown on pg. 47. Sew together according to the diagram, sewing from the edge of each point to the inside seam allowance and backstitching. Set in a teardrop unit and a half-diamond as shown. This completes one border unit. Make 13 more of these.

8. Cut from muslin:
- sixteen 3" triangles
- four 5¼" triangles
- four triangle halves cut from 3½" triangles
- four triangle halves cut from 5¾" triangles

Using these pieces, the extra pieced triangles from #3, and all of the border units, assemble two short borders and two long borders. Finish the ends of the short borders with the 3½" and 5¾" muslin triangle halves as shown. Finish the long borders with 7¼" squares of muslin cut to a 60° angle as shown in the diagram. Matching centers and edges, sew on the two short borders. Measure the length of the quilt top at the center and left and right edges and trim the two long borders to this length, trimming equal amounts from each end. Sew on the two long borders. The author added a final 8" muslin border.

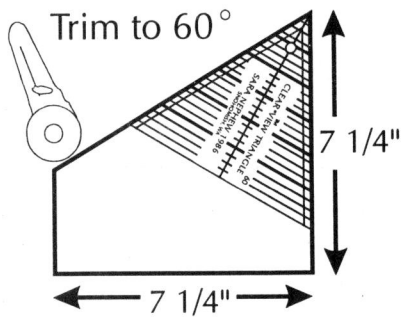

Trim to 60°

7 1/4"

7 1/4"

English Rose
With A Wild Rose Border

POSITIVELY PANSY *(from a design by Caryl Steimel)*

1¾" triangle
Quilt with borders: 84" x 92¾"

All fabrics prewashed 42" wide.
Fabric requirements:
¾ yd. pink
1 yd. purple
½ yd. yellow
⅓ yd. black
1¾ yd. green
6½ yds. muslin

Directions:
1. Cut for one pansy wedge:
- 2 pink 2¾" triangles
- 2 pink flat pyramids cut from 1½" strip at 2¾" on the Clearview Triangle
- 2 purple 2¾" triangles
- 4 muslin 1¾" triangles
- 2 muslin flat pyramids cut from a 1½" strip at 3¾" on the Clearview Triangle
- 2 purple hexagons cut from a 2½" strip (cut a 2½" diamond, then cut a 1¼" triangle from each end)

2. Sandwich piece 1¾" strips of purple and yellow and cut 24 matching triangles (one set of strips). Sandwich piece 1¾" strips of black and yellow and cut 72 matching triangles (three sets of strips).

3. To strip-piece Stem Diamonds cut:
- 1½" muslin strip
- 1" green strip
- 1" muslin strip
Sew into a 2½" set of strips as shown. Cut diamonds from the set of strips. Be sure to cut the diamonds in the right direction, so the stem is placed as shown.

4. Assemble the pansy in order as follows:

A. sew one purple, four yellow, and three black 1¾" triangles into a diamond that is the pansy face. Then add two pink flat pyramids as shown to make a gem shape.

B. Use the purple hexagons, the muslin 1¾" triangles, and the purple 2¾" triangles to make the left and right pansy cheeks. Sew the stem diamond to one of the cheeks to make a strip. Sew the face to the other cheek and seam both sections together.

C. Sew the muslin flat pyramids to the remaining 2¾" pink triangles and add these at left and right to complete the pansy wedge. Make 24 of these.

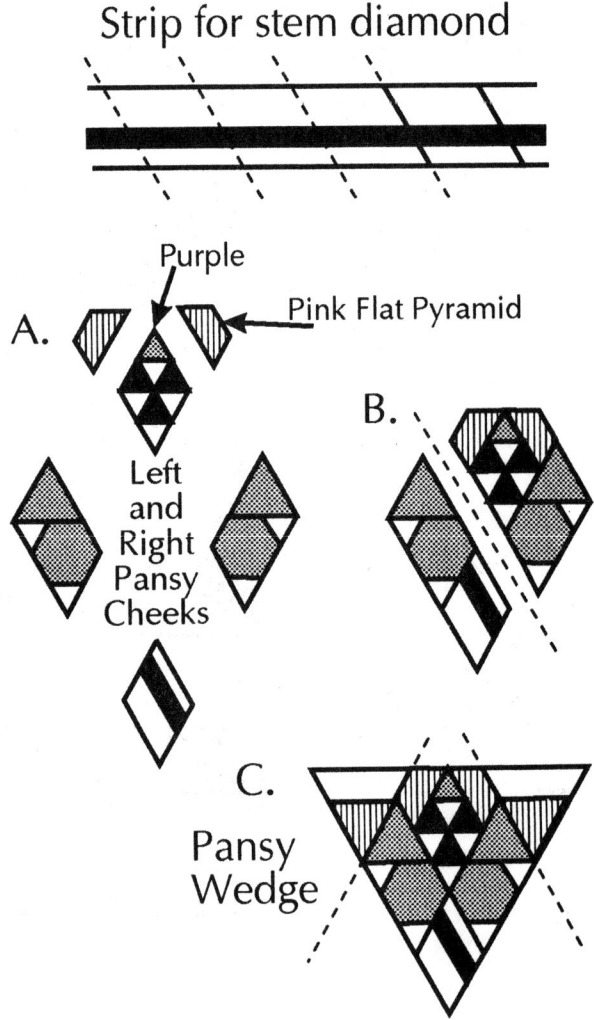

Strip for stem diamond

Purple

Pink Flat Pyramid

A.

Left and Right Pansy Cheeks

B.

C.

Pansy Wedge

Positively Pansy

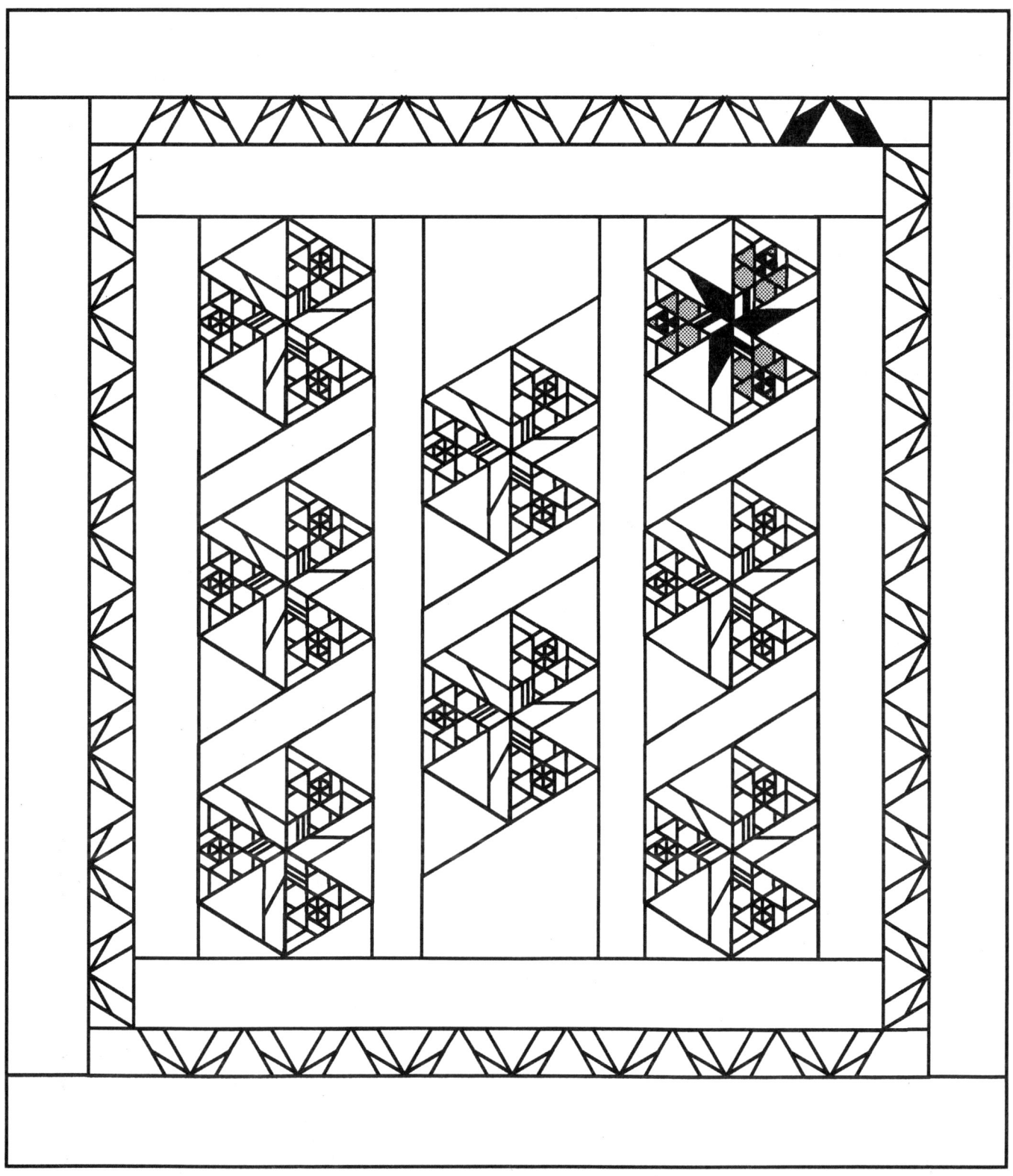

5. Cut for the leaf wedge:
- 1 muslin 6¾" triangle
- 1 muslin special shape (cut a flat pyramid from a 2½" strip at 7⅜" on the Clearview Triangle--then trim the **right** end to a 30° angle as shown)
- 1 green special shape ((cut a flat pyramid from a 2½" strip at 7⅜" on the Clearview Triangle--then trim the **left** end to a 30° angle as shown)

Note: the special shapes do have a reverse. If you are working with prints, be sure to turn all the flat pyramids right side up before trimming the end to a 30° angle.

Sew the muslin and green special shapes together into a strip. Offset the two 30° angles enough so the seam falls in the notch and the pieces line up straight when the seam is pressed to the dark. Practice will make this easier. Then sew on the muslin 6¾" triangle to complete the leaf wedge. Make 24 of these.

6. Sew three pansy wedges and three leaf wedges into half-block A and half-block B, pressing seams as indicated. Sew the two halves together to make a hexagon. Make eight of these. Cut 12 muslin 8¾" triangles. Sew two of these on opposite sides of four pansy hexagons as shown to make complete *PANSY* blocks.

In the quilt, blocks are all oriented with a Pansy wedge in the upper right. As you make the corner blocks and sew the top together, check to make sure all the blocks are in the correct direction.

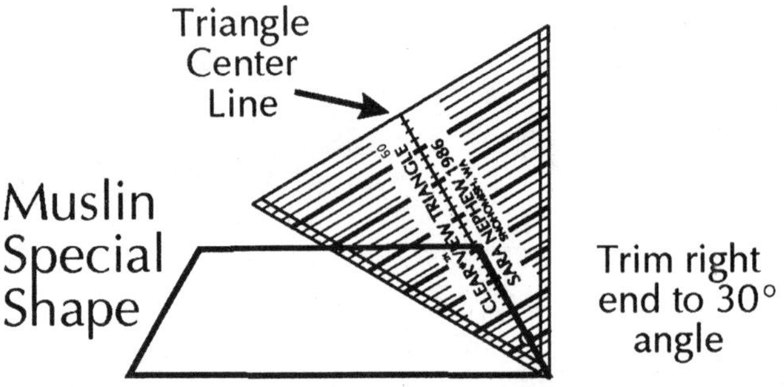

Muslin Special Shape

Triangle Center Line

Trim right end to 30° angle

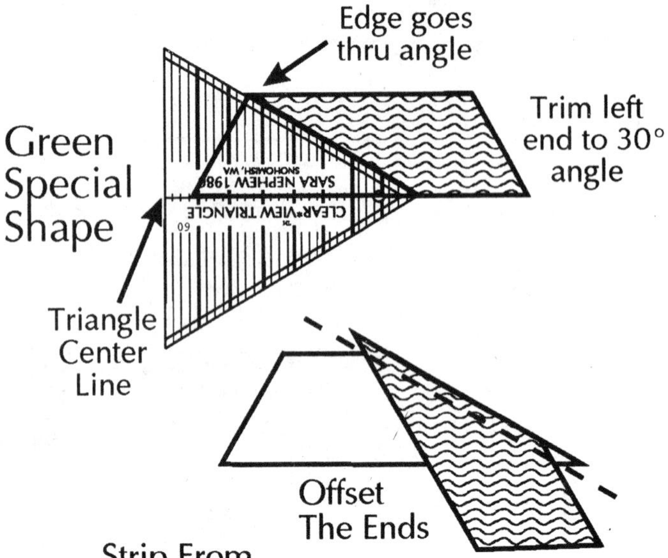

Green Special Shape

Edge goes thru angle

Trim left end to 30° angle

Triangle Center Line

Offset The Ends

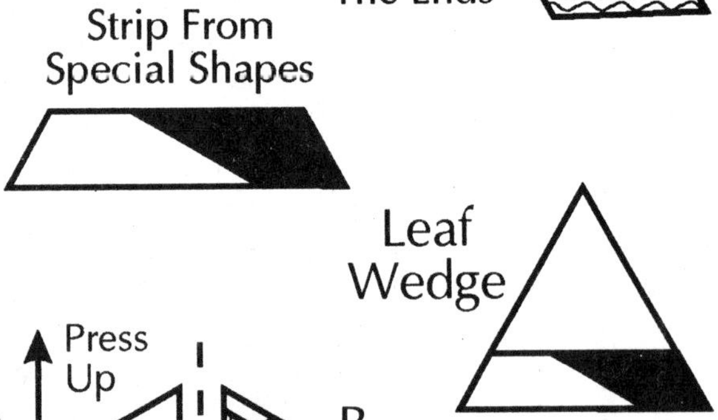

Strip From Special Shapes

Leaf Wedge

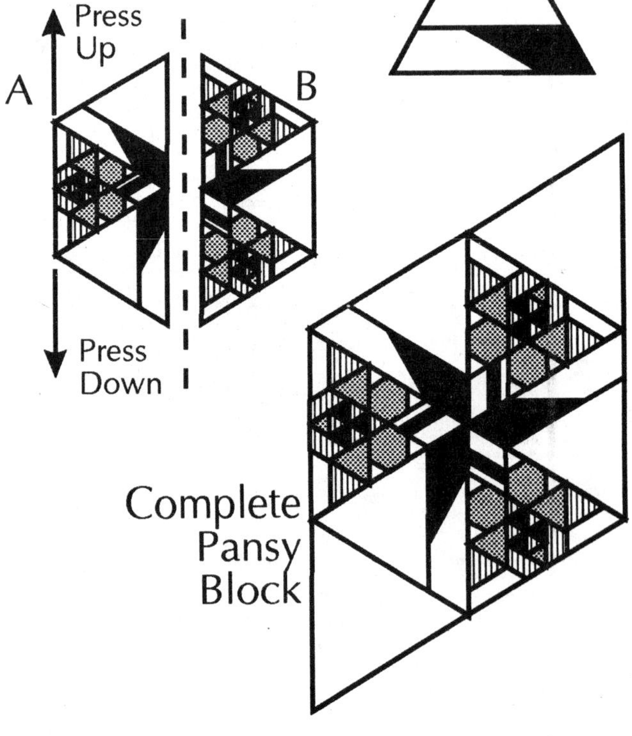

A Press Up B Press Down

Complete Pansy Block

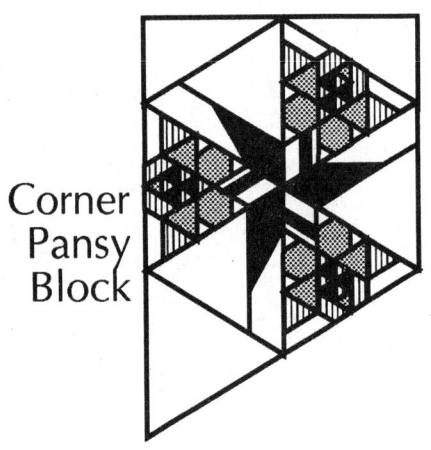

Corner Pansy Block

7. Cut four muslin 9¼" triangles and bisect to make eight 9¼" triangle halves. Sew the triangle halves and the remaining four 8¾" triangles onto the last four pansy hexagons to make four corner blocks.

8. From muslin cut:
- a 16½" selvage-to-selvage width, cut again in half to make two 16½" x 21" rectangles
- 4½" setting strips (cut one end to a 60° angle, sew onto a block, then trim the other end to line up with the block)

Sew the two outside rows, each with two corner blocks, setting strips, and one complete block. For the center row, sew two blocks together with a setting strip. Then trim one end of each 16½" x 21" muslin rectangle to a 60° angle as shown. Sew this fill-in-piece at the top and bottom of the center row. Measure the two outside rows and trim the center row to match by taking an equal amount off the top and bottom. Sew all three rows together with 4½" muslin setting strips between. Add a 5" inner border of muslin at the top and bottom and a 5¼" muslin border at left and right.

9. To piece the pansy leaf border cut:
- 56 muslin 4⅝" triangles
- 28 green special shapes as in #4 above
- 28 green reverse special shapes
- 56 muslin diamond halves from 1¾" strip

Sew the green special shape and the muslin diamond half into a strip as shown. Sew the reverse special shape and the muslin diamond half into a reverse strip. Using a strip, a reverse strip, and a muslin triangle, make a pansy scallop as shown. Sew the scallops into a border row, placing another muslin triangle between each scallop. Use eight scallops in each left and right border, and seven units in each top and bottom border. For a fancy corner, just match and pin centers and ends of the borders to the quilt top and seam on each side. For a square corner finish the ends of the left and right borders with a 5" muslin triangle half cut from a 5" triangle. Finish the ends of top and bottom borders with a 4½" x 7" muslin rectangle trimmed to a 60° angle (and its reverse, place fabrics right sides together before cutting). Add a 4¾" muslin border.

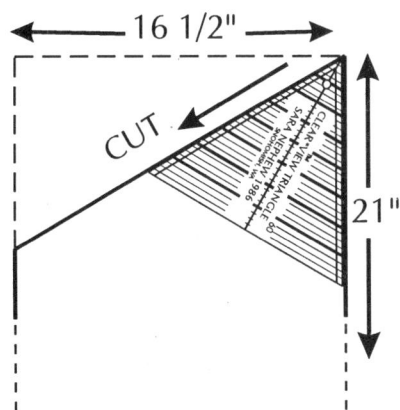

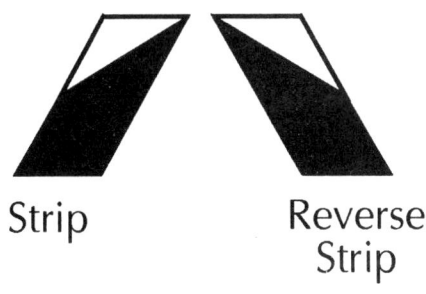

Strip   Reverse Strip

Pansy Scallop

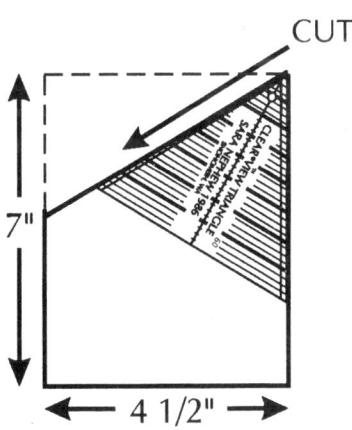

PANSY GARDEN *(from a design by Caryl Steimel)*

1 ¾" triangle
Quilt with borders:
65 ¾" x 79"

All fabric prewashed 42" wide.
Fabric requirements:
⅓ yd. purple
⅓ yd. blue
⅓ yd. pink
⅛ yd. yellow
⅛ yd. black
1 ¼ yd. green
5 ¾ yds. peach

Directions:

1. Cut for one pansy wedge:
* 2 pink 2 ¾" triangles
* 2 pink flat pyramids cut from 1 ½" strip at 2 ¾" on the Clearview Triangle
* 1 purple and 1 blue 2 ¾" triangle
* 4 peach 1 ¾" triangles
* 2 peach flat pyramids cut from a 1 ½" strip at 3 ¾" on the Clearview Triangle
* 1 purple and 1 blue hexagon cut from a 2 ½" strip (cut a 2 ½" diamond, then cut a 1 ¼" triangle from each end)

2. Sandwich piece 1 ¾" strips of blue and yellow and cut 13 matching triangles (one set of strips). Sandwich piece 1 ¾" strips of black and yellow and cut 39 matching triangles (one set of strips).

3. To strip-piece Stem Diamonds cut:
* 1 ½" peach strip
* 1" green strip
* 1" peach strip
Sew into a 2 ½" set of strips as shown. Cut diamonds from the set of strips. Be sure to cut the diamonds in the right direction, so the stem is placed as shown on pg. 54.

4. Make 13 pansy wedges and 26 leaf wedges as on pgs.54-56. Sew into 13 of Pansy Half-block A (diagram on pg. 56).

5. Cut from peach:
* eight 8 ¾" triangles
* six 9 ¼" triangle halves from 9 ¼" triangles

6. Assemble a row from three half-blocks and two peach triangles, finishing each end with a triangle half. Make two more of these rows.

7. Assemble a row from two half-blocks, one peach triangle, and two 8 ½" x 14 ½" peach rectangles trimmed to a 60° angle as shown and the reverse (put right sides together before cutting). Make another of these rows.

8. Sew the rows together with a 4 ½" peach setting strip cut to the same length as all the rows. Add a top and bottom 7 ½" peach border.

9. To add the Mock Scallop border: Cut peach diamond halves from a 2 ¾" strip. Cut green diamond halves from a 1 ¾" strip. Sew together as in the diagram to make a mock scallop. Sew the mock scallops (7 top and bottom and 9 left and right) and 2 ¾" peach triangles into the borders. Finish the ends of the left and right borders with 3 ¼" peach triangle halves from 3 ¼" triangles. Finish each end of the top and bottom borders with a 2 ¾" x 4" peach rectangle trimmed to a 60° angle and its reverse (put right sides together before cutting). Add a final 2 ½" peach border.

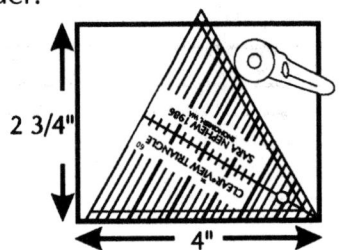

Pansy Garden

GRAPES

1½" triangle
Quilt with borders: 79¼" x 91"
All fabric prewashed 42" wide.
Fabric requirements:
7¾ yds. muslin
1½ yds. green
¾ yds. grape fabrics (eight assorted 2" strips)

Directions:
1. To strip piece the stem diamond cut and sew together into a set of strips:
- 1¼" muslin strip
- 1" green strip
- ¾" muslin strip

Cut diamonds from the set of strips. You will need 18 altogether.

2. Cut for each bunch of grapes;
- 8 hexagons from a 2" strip
- 16 muslin 1 ½" triangles
- 1 muslin long diamond cut from a 3" strip at 5" on the Clearview Triangle
- 1 stem diamond

Assemble according to the diagram.

3. Cut for each leaf:
- 1 muslin 5¼" triangle
- 2 sets of green and muslin matching triangles cut from 3" strips
- 1 green flat pyramid cut from a 2" strip at 3¾" on the Clearview Triangle
- 4 muslin 2¼" triangles
- 1 green and white matching triangle cut from 2¼" strips

Assemble according to the diagram.

4. Sew grape section and leaf section together as shown to make a complete block. Make 18 blocks altogether.

TO ASSEMBLE THE QUILT TOP:

5.. Cut from muslin:
- 11 long diamonds from 7½" strips at 14¾" line on the Clearview Triangle
- 4 muslin rectangles 6" x 10¼"
- 6 muslin 7½" x 17" rectangles

Cut small muslin rectangles diagonally as shown to produce eight 10¼" triangle halves. Trim one end of the large muslin rectangles to a 60° angle to produce a finishing piece.

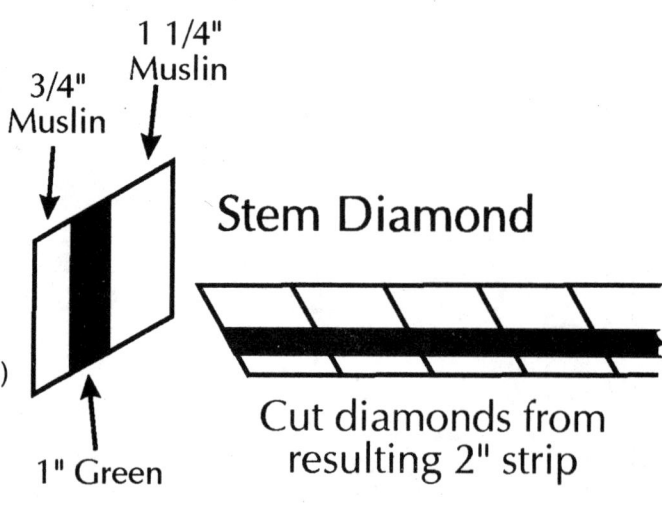

3/4" Muslin

1 1/4" Muslin

Stem Diamond

Cut diamonds from resulting 2" strip

1" Green

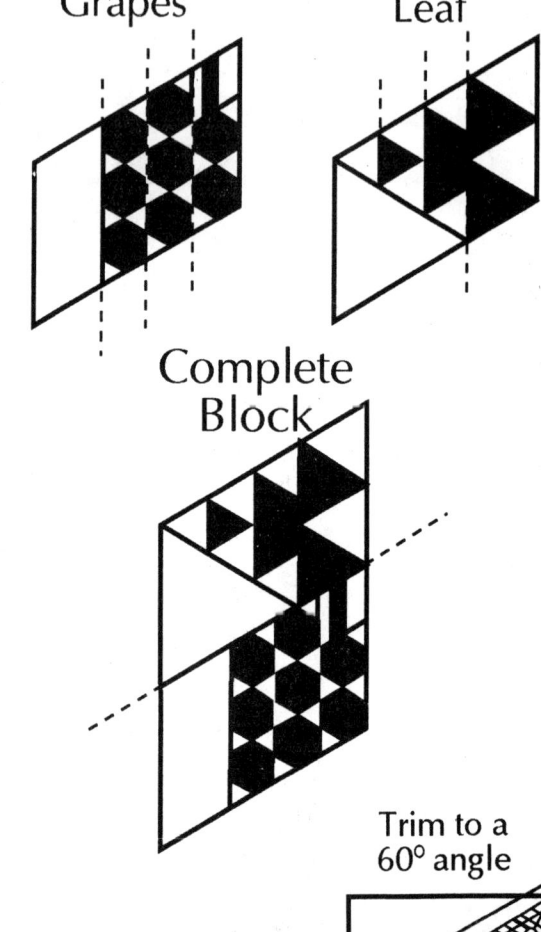

Grapes

Leaf

Complete Block

Trim to a 60° angle

6"

10 1/4"

Grapes

6. Rows 1, 3, 5, and 7 are assembled from three blocks, two muslin diamonds, and two 10¼" muslin triangle halves. Rows 2, 4, and 6 are assembled from two blocks, one muslin diamond, and two finishing pieces. Add a 7¼" muslin border on all four sides as shown in the quilt diagram.

GRAPE LEAF BORDER:

7. Sandwich piece 112 pairs of 3" matching triangles from green and muslin. (6 sets of strips) Sew into four rows of matching triangles, each containing 28 pairs. Remove one white triangle so the border ends with a green triangle at left and right. Then sew onto each end a muslin triangle half cut from a 3½" triangle.

8. Cut 56 green and 60 muslin flat pyramids from a 2" strip at 3¾" on the Clearview Triangle. You may want to stack and cut up to four strips at the same time. Sew into four second border rows of alternate flat pyramids, each containing fourteen green flat pyramids. At left and right, finish this second border with muslin flat pyramids.

9. Cut 56 green triangles from 2¼" strips. Cut 60 muslin flat pyramids from 2" strips at 5¼" on the Clearview Triangle. Sew into four third border rows, alternating 14 triangles and 15 flat pyramids, and ending the row at left and right with muslin flat pyramids.

10. Sew the three border rows together to produce four complete borders. To make the leaf, center each piece over the green piece(s) in the previous row. Trim the ends of the second and third border rows even with the edge of the muslin triangle half. Sew on the two side borders, matching centers and ends. Then sew on the top and bottom borders, matching centers and ends. Add a final 3" muslin border.

First Border Row

Second Border Row

Third Border Row

Grape Leaf Border

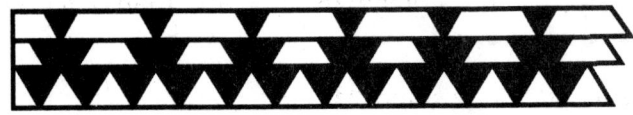

MIXED FRUIT
1¾" triangle
Quilt with borders: 58½" x 69½"

All fabric prewashed 42" wide.
Fabric requirements:
4¾ yds. background fabric
¼ yd. cherry fabric
½ yd. light green fabric
⅔yd. grape fabric
1 yd. dark green fabric
¼ yd. stem fabric

Directions:
1. Make five blocks of *Grapes* according to the directions below. Cut for one bunch of grapes:
- 8 hexagons of grape fabric cut from a 2½" strip (cut a 2½" diamond and cut a 1¼" triangle from each end)
- 16 background 1¾" triangles

Sew the triangles to the hexagons and sew into three rows as shown. Do not sew the rows together.

2. Cut:
- 1½" strip of background fabric
- 1" strip of stem fabric
- 1" strip of background fabric

(Use half of a selvage-to-selvage cut. Save and cut down the other half to make the cherry stems.)

Cut 2½" diamonds as shown from the set of strips. Add one stem diamond to the short row of hexagons and sew the three rows together. Cut five background long diamonds as shown (the long diamond does have a reverse of its shape, so be sure you are cutting the correct piece) from a 3½" strip at 6½" on the Clearview Triangle. Sew onto the left side of the grapes as shown.

3. Sandwich piece 28 matching triangles from a 3¾" set of strips (dark green and background fabric). Then also cut for each grape leaf:
- 5 background 2¾" triangles
- 1 dark green 2¾" triangle
- 1 dark green flat pyramid cut from a 2½" strip at 4¾" on the Clearview Triangle
- 1 background 6¾" triangle

Add two matching triangles and assemble into a grape leaf section as shown. Sew onto the bunch of grapes to make a complete block.

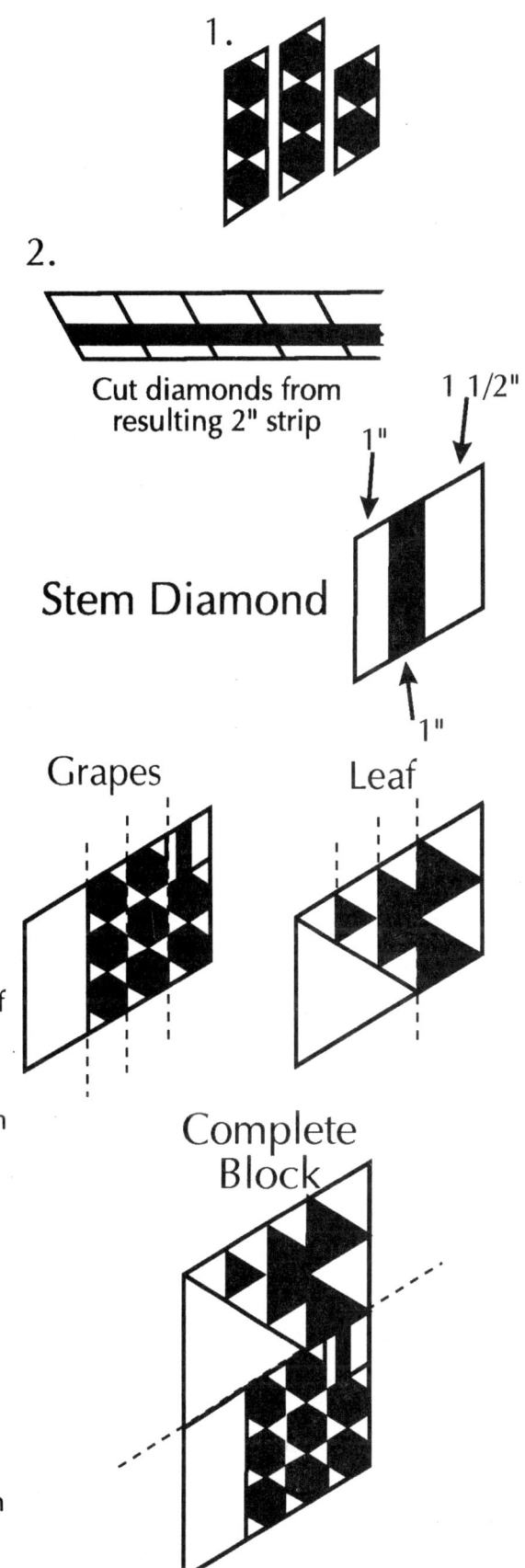

1.

2.

Cut diamonds from resulting 2" strip

1 1/2"

1"

1"

Stem Diamond

1"

Grapes

Leaf

Complete Block

4. Make four blocks of *Cherries* according to the directions on pg. 41-42. Cut four background long diamonds from a 2½" strip at 6½" on the Clearview Triangle. Seam onto the left side of each *Cherries* block as shown.

To assemble the quilt top:
5. Cut:
- 6 background long diamonds from a 4½" strip at 9½" on the Clearview Triangle
- 4 background 10" triangle halves (cut two rectangles 5¾" x 10" and bisect as shown)
- 2 background finishing pieces (cut two squares 9½" x 9½" and trim to a 60° angle as shown)

Use these pieces and all the blocks to make three vertical rows. Put the triangle halves at the top and bottom of the left and right rows and the finishing pieces at the top and bottom of the center row. Trim the center row evenly top and bottom to match the length of the other two rows.

6. Sew the rows together using 4½" setting strips if background fabric (measure to the same length as the three rows). Add a 3½" inner border of background fabric top and bottom, and a 4¾" inner border of background fabric left and right.

To piece the *Mixed Fruit* border:
7. Cut for the inside ⅔ of the border:
- 36 background diamonds from a 2½" strip
- 18 dark green flat pyramids cut from a 2½" strip at 4¾" on the Clearview Triangle

Use these pieces and the remaining matching triangles from #3 to sew into a partial leaf as shown. Make 18 of these. Then cut 14 background flat pyramids from a 5½" strip at 7¾" on the Clearview Triangle. From 8 partial leaves and 6 background flat pyramids make the top and bottom borders as shown. Finish the ends with triangle halves cut from 6¼" triangles. Sew onto the quilt top. From 10 partial leaves and eight background flat pyramids make the left and right borders as shown. Finish both ends with 5½" x 8" background rectangles trimmed to 60° angles as shown. (two and two reverse) Don't sew these left and right borders onto the quilt top yet.

Cherries Block

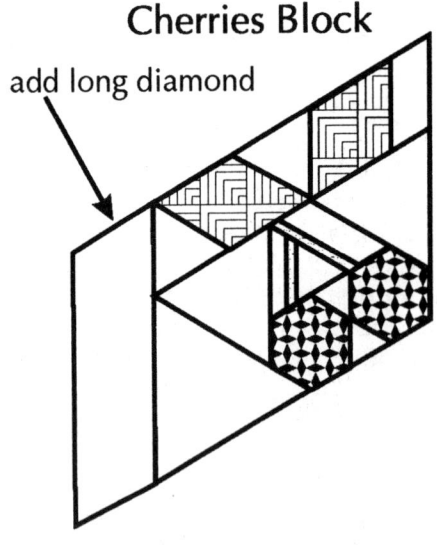

add long diamond

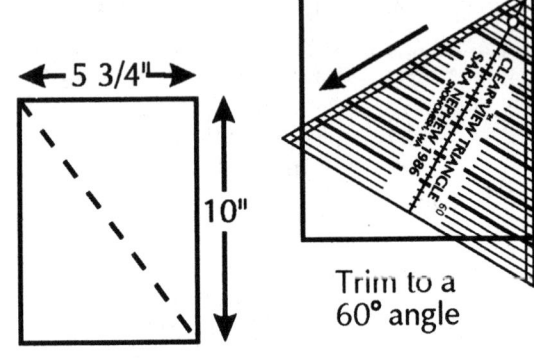

←5 3/4"→

10"

Trim to a 60° angle

7.

Partial Leaf

Top and Bottom Border

Left and Right Border

Mixed Fruit

8. Cut a 2½" strip of light green and of background fabric. Sew into a set of strips as shown. Press the seam to the dark, and then fold the strip right sides together. Cut the end to a 60° angle, and then cut 2½" sections, checking the angle often. This will give you a pieced long diamond and its reverse. Cut 17 of each. Cut 22 background 2¾" triangles and 18 dark green 2¾" triangles. Sew with the strip-pieced long diamonds to assemble the final pieced border. Finish the ends of the left and right final borders with triangle halves cut from background 3¼" triangles. Add these to the left and right borders and sew them as a unit onto the quilt top. Finish the top and bottom final borders with a background 2½" x 4" rectangle and its reverse (place right sides together) trimmed to a 60° angle. Sew on, matching centers to complete the leaves.

8.   Set of Strips

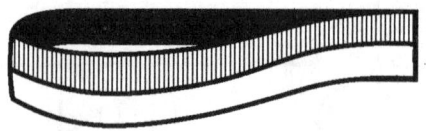

Fold right sides together

Trim to 60° angle

← Fold

Cut 2 1/2" sections

← Fold

to get left and
Right Long Diamonds

Final Left and Right Border

Side Border Unit

BABY ROSE

2" triangle size
Quilt with borders: 35" x 35¼"

All fabric prewashed 42" wide.
Fabric requirements:
2½ yds. white-on-white muslin
½ yd. red fabric
¾ yd. green fabric

Directions:
1. Piece one block of *Peppermint Rose*:
Sandwich piece 18 half-diamonds from a
1¼" set of strips. Cut six light 2" triangles.
Assemble a gem shape in strips as shown.
Make six of these gem shapes.

2. Sew the gem shapes together three and
three, pressing the seams as shown. (Butt the
seams at the center tips, put under the
presser foot, sew from the inside edge to the
seam allowance and backstitch.) Then sew
the two halves together, matching the centers
and pinning. Sew from Seam allowance to
seam allowance, backstitching. Press the
center seam open about an inch where all 12
seams come together.

3. From two muslin triangle halves and one red
gem shape make a teardrop unit. Make five more
of these. Set in the teardrop units around the
outside edge of the seamed gem shapes. Make
two *Peppermint Rose* blocks altogether.

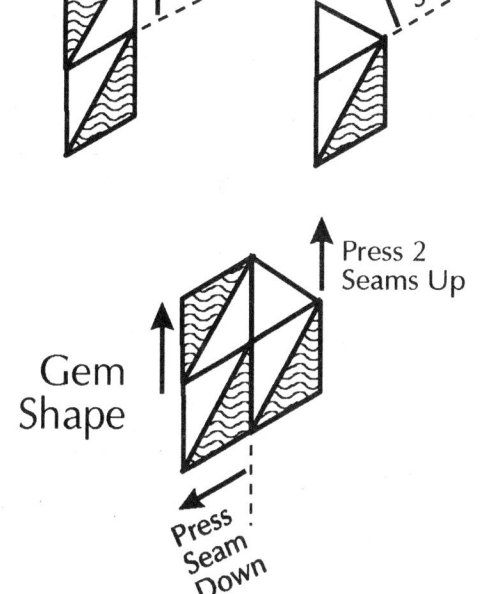

Press Seam Up

Press Seam Up

Gem Shape

Press 2 Seams Up

Press Seam Down

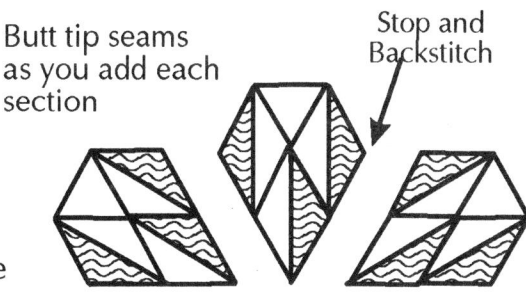

Butt tip seams
as you add each
section

Stop and
Backstitch

Inside Edge

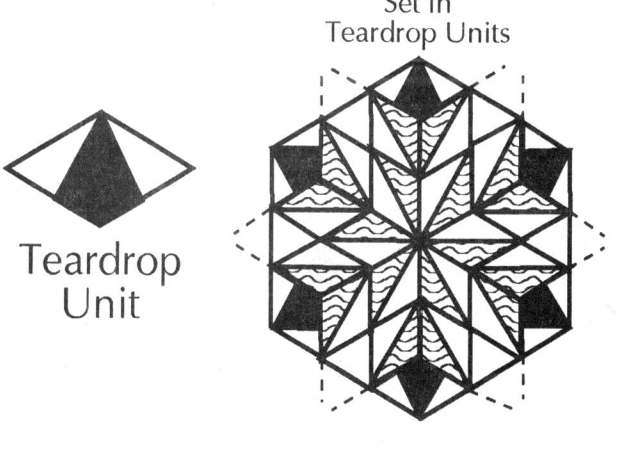

Teardrop
Unit

Set in
Teardrop Units

Peppermint Rose
Block

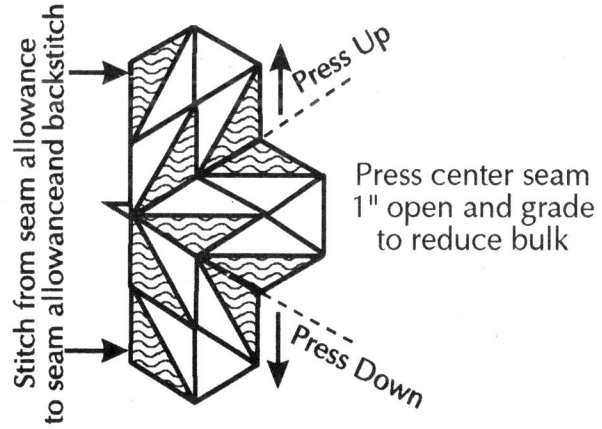

Stitch from seam allowance
to seam allowance and backstitch

Press Up

Press center seam
1" open and grade
to reduce bulk

Press Down

4. Piece one block of Cabbage Rose:
Sandwich piece six half-triangles from 1½"
red and muslin strips. Sew three and three to
make the center of the flower. Cut six red 2"
triangles. Sew three triangles onto the center
hexagon to make the center triangle.
Sandwich piece six half-diamonds from a
1¼" red and muslin set of strips. From one
triangle and two half-diamonds make a strip
as shown. Make two more of these strips.
Sew the strips onto the center triangle to
make a second hexagon.

5. Cut 12 green and six muslin 2" triangles.
Sew two green and one muslin triangle(s)
into a flat pyramid shape as shown. Make
five more of these. Sew three of these flat
pyramid shapes onto three separate sides of
the second hexagon to make a larger triangle.

 6. Piece six red and muslin teardrop units.
From two teardrop units and one flat pyramid
make a strip as shown. Make two more of
these. Sew this strip onto each side of the
larger triangle to make a hexagon again.

Make two *Cabbage Rose* blocks altogether.

Assemble the top:

7. Cut eight muslin 4½" triangles and seam them
to the four blocks as shown to make diamond
shapes. Make two rows as shown, with a 2"
setting strip between the blocks. (Trim the end of
the strip to a 60° angle, sew onto the block, and
trim the other end even with the block edge.)
Finish the top and bottom of each row with an
muslin triangle half cut from an 8¼" triangle.
Sew the rows together with three 3⅛" muslin
setting strips as shown. (Measure the rows and
make the setting strips the same length.)

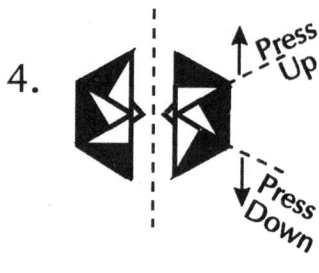

4.

4.

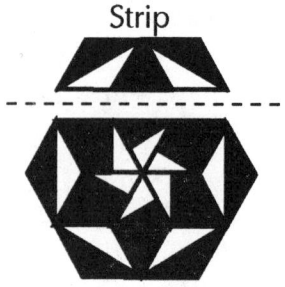

Triangle

Strip

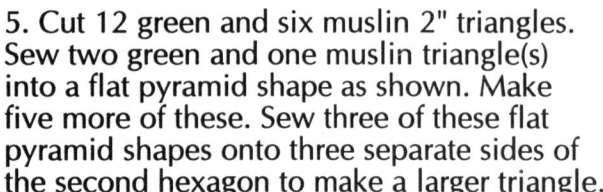

Flat Pyramid

5.

Larger Triangle

Teardrop Unit

Cabbage Rose Block

6.

Baby Rose

For the *Wild Rose* border:

8. To make one border unit:
Sandwich-piece five green and muslin half-diamonds from a 1¼" set of strips. (You will need 100 half-diamonds altogether.)
Piece two teardrop units as shown from red 2¼" teardrops and muslin 2½" triangle halves. (40 altogether) Cut two 2" muslin triangles. (72 altogether) Cut one muslin diamond.(20 altogether)

Sew four half-diamonds, one muslin diamond, and one teardrop unit into three rows as shown. Sew together according to the diagram, sewing from the edge of each point to the inside seam allowance and backstitching. Set in a teardrop unit and a half-diamond as shown. (The author finger pressed this piece until the whole unit was complete, and then used a wet press cloth, pressing from the front and letting the seams twist on the back.)

Make 20 border units altogether.

9. Cut eight green diamonds from a 1¾" strip. Sew two muslin triangles to each diamond as shown to make a pieced triangle. Cut four 3¼" muslin triangles. From two pieced triangles, a 3¼" muslin triangle, five 2" muslin triangles, and five border units, assemble a complete *Wild Rose* side border as shown. Make three more of these. Finish the ends of the left and right borders with two muslin triangle halves cut from a 2½" triangle and two muslin triangle halves cut from a 3¾" triangle. Finish the ends of the top and bottom borders with a 4¼" x 4¾" rectangle trimmed to a 60° angle as shown. Add a final 2½" muslin border. (Measure centers and edges of the quilt top to find the border lengths.)

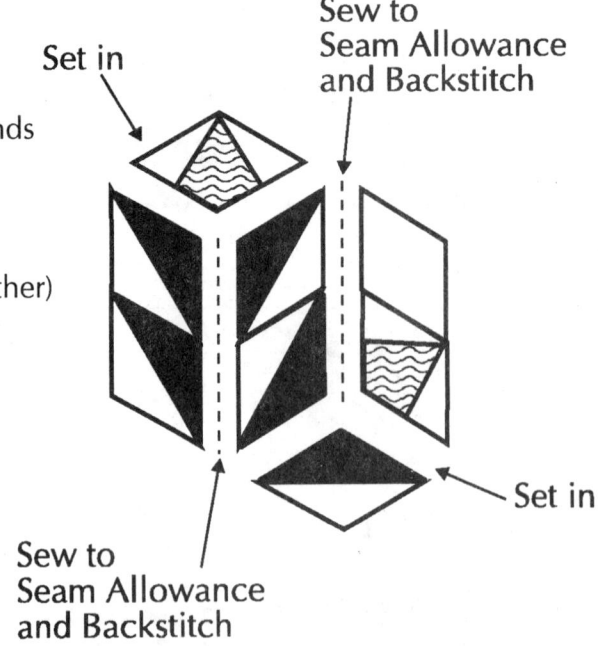

Set in

Sew to Seam Allowance and Backstitch

Sew to Seam Allowance and Backstitch

Set in

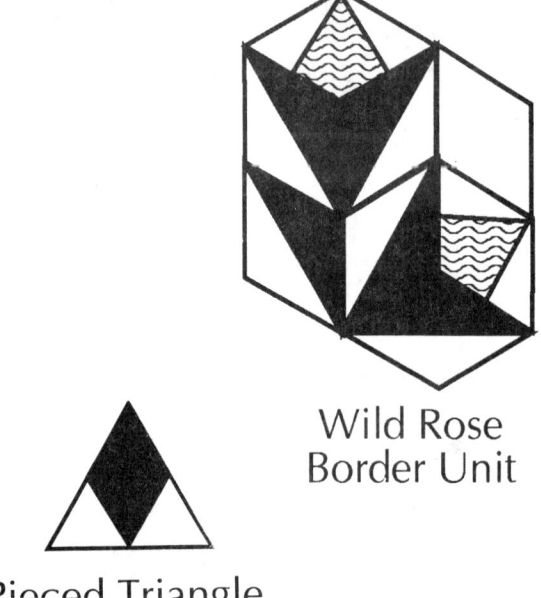

Wild Rose Border Unit

Pieced Triangle

Wild Rose Side Border

Piecing Hints

- Check your seams occasionally. The seam should be scant (just inside ¼" line instead of on it).

- When constructing half-diamonds or teardrops, the quilter may wish to cut a fabric diamond according to the rules, and lay it over these seamed pieces to see if they are the correct size. The pieces can be trimmed, or seam allowances could be adjusted if necessary.

- Press to the dark when possible as you construct each block. Press from the top with a wet press cloth when a block is complete--then turn it over and check the back for unattractive seams.

- Plan quilting to avoid seams as much as possible. Equilateral quilts will have more bulk at seam intersections (six seams coming together).

- Keep the ink side down when using Clearview Triangle (and all other) rulers, to increase accuracy. (This avoids parallax.)

- To avoid bulky seam intersections, it is often a good idea to allow a seam to twist.

- At a point where many seams intersect, pinch together at the back and open from the front to see how the seams match. Then pin.

- Trim long (rabbit or donkey) seam ears as soon as possible (found on half-diamonds, diamond halves, half-triangles, triangle halves) but leave short seam ears (kitty or puppy) as keys for matching seams until after the top is constructed.

- If the seaming and pressing results in a triangle of fabric lying across the seam, insert the scissors between layers (so the little triangle sticking out over the edge is not removed) and trim off the excess fabric at an angle as shown. Stay about ⅛" away from the seam intersection. This greatly reduces bulk. (see diagrams 1 & 2 below)

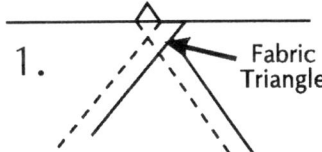

1. Fabric Triangle

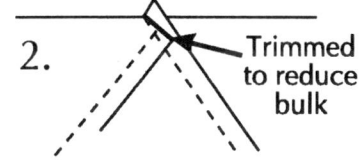

2. Trimmed to reduce bulk

Index of Cutting and Piecing

About the Author

Sara Nephew began her artistry in metalwork. After receiving her B.A. as an Art Major, she worked for a commercial shop, designing and repairing jewelry, and invented a new enamel-on-brass technique. Her cloisonne' work appeared in national exhibits.

She has since turned her interests to quilting, in large part because of the many attractions of fabric. Sara is the originator of a series of tools for rotary cutting isometric shapes, and is an internationally known teacher.

Sara is the author of six previous quilting books. **Quilts From a Different Angle** was an introduction to 60° triangle quilts. **My Mother's Quilts: Designs From the Thirties** helped inspire renewed interest in depression-era quilts. **Stars and Flowers: Three-sided Patchwork** introduced concentric 60° designs, some of which looked like floral applique'. **Building Block Quilts** and **Building Block Quilts 2** explored isometric 3-D illusions. And **Easy and Elegant Quilts** showed the design possibilities of 60° shapes used in one and two-patch quilts. With three friends, Sara also co-authored a book on rotary cut triangle quilts, **Quick and Easy Quiltmaking**.

Sara lives in Clearview, Washington, with her husband Dale. They have three children and one grandchild.

Available from Clearview Triangle

60° 6" Clearview Triangle -- ruled every ¼"	$ 6.50	plus $1.50 sh*
60° 12" Clearview Triangle -- ruled every ¼"	$11.50	plus $2.00 sh*
60° 8" Mini-Pro -- ruled every ⅛"	$ 9.50	plus $1.75 sh*
120° Half-Diamond -- ruled every ⅛"	$10.50	plus $2.00 sh*
2-sided Graph Paper Pad -- 30 sheets	$ 5.95	plus $1.00 sh*
Stars and Flowers: Three-sided Patchwork	$12.95	plus $2.00 sh*
Building Block Quilts	$14.95	plus $2.00 sh*
Building Block Quilts 2	$14.95	plus $2.00 sh*
Easy and Elegant Quilts	$15.95	plus $2.00 sh*

* Subtract $1.00 from shipping for each item after the first.

Order From: Clearview Triangle, Dept. 4
8311 180th St. S.E.
Snohomish, WA, 98290-4802   USA